FORTRESS • 92

STRONGHOLDS OF THE PICTS

The fortifications of Dark Age Scotland

ANGUS KONSTAM

ILLUSTRATED BY PETER DENNIS

Series editors Marcus Cowper and Nikolai Bogdanovic

First published in 2010 by Osprey Publishing
Midland House, West Way, Botley, Oxford OX2 0PH, UK
44-02 23rd St, Suite 219, Long Island City, NY 11101, USA
E-mail: info@ospreypublishing.com

ISBN 978 1 84603 686 6
E-book ISBN 978 1 84908 257 0

Editorial by Ilios Publishing Ltd, Oxford, UK (www.iliospublishing.com)
Cartography: Map Studio, Romsey, UK
Page layout by Ken Vail Graphic Design, Cambridge, UK (kvgd.com)
Typeset in Myriad and Sabon
Index by Alan Thatcher
Originated by United Graphic Pte Ltd, Singapore
Printed in China throught Bookbuilders

10 11 12 13 14   10 9 8 7 6 5 4 3 2 1

A CIP catalogue record for this book is available from the British Library.

EDITOR'S NOTE

Unless otherwise indicated all images belong to the Stratford Archive.

ARTIST'S NOTE

Readers may care to note that the original paintings from which the
colour plates in this book were prepared are available for private sale.
All reproduction copyright whatsoever is retained by the Publishers.
All enquiries should be addressed to:

Peter Dennis, Fieldhead, The Park, Mansfield, Notts, NG18 2AT, UK

The Publishers regret that they can enter into no correspondence upon
this matter.

THE FORTRESS STUDY GROUP (FSG)

The object of the FSG is to advance the education of the public in the
study of all aspects of fortifications and their armaments, especially works
constructed to mount or resist artillery. The FSG holds an annual
conference in September over a long weekend with visits and evening
lectures, an annual tour abroad lasting about eight days, and an annual
Members' Day.

The FSG journal FORT is published annually, and its newsletter Casemate is
published three times a year. Membership is international. For further
details, please contact:

The Secretary, c/o 6 Lanark Place, London W9 1BS, UK

Website: www.fsgfort.com

THE WOODLAND TRUST

Osprey Publishing are supporting the Woodland Trust, the UK's leading
woodland conservation charity, by funding the dedication of trees.

FOR A CATALOGUE OF ALL BOOKS PUBLISHED BY OSPREY MILITARY
AND AVIATION PLEASE CONTACT:

Osprey Direct, c/o Random House Distribution Center,
400 Hahn Road, Westminster, MD 21157
E-mail: uscustomerservice@ospreypublishing.com

Osprey Direct, The Book Service Ltd, Distribution Centre,
Colchester Road, Frating Green, Colchester, Essex, CO7 7DW
E-mail: customerservice@ospreypublishing.com

www.ospreypublishing.com

CONTENTS

STRONGHOLDS OF THE PICTS
THE EARLY HISTORIC FORTS OF SCOTLAND

INTRODUCTION

The Picts have long been a historical enigma. In 1955 a long-awaited academic study of the Early Historic inhabitants of northern Scotland was published. The book's editor Dr F. T. Wainwright was quite frank about the lack of available evidence. For generations, scholars had been baffled by these enigmatic people and the scant legacy they left behind them. Appropriately enough, Wainwright called his book *The Problem of the Picts*.

While the book was something of a milestone, many important problems remained unresolved. Scholars were still unable to agree on what language these people spoke, what the meaning of their strange carved stones was, or even what happened to them. Over the past 50 years a significant body of new archaeological and historical information has been unearthed. This greatly improves our knowledge of the Picts, and their fellow inhabitants of the land we now know as Scotland. Important new studies have been written, and some of these have even tackled the way these Dark Age peoples fought their enemies, and showed how they relied on fortifications to dominate the countryside.

The Picts certainly needed strongholds. For a people on the edge of the known world they seemed to be surrounded by enemies. To the south-west lay the Britons of Strathclyde, whose kings ruled from the imposing fortress of Alt Clut (now Dumbarton). The Britons to the south-east were less able to defend themselves, and eventually their lands were conquered by a newcomer – the Angles of Northumbria – whose territory soon extended as far north as present day Edinburgh (then called Dun Eidin). Another threat appeared from the west in the form of the Scots of Dal Riata – Irish settlers who soon carved out a homeland in Argyll, anchored on the stronghold of Dunadd.

In the centuries before the coming of the Romans the hill fort was an important element in Celtic British society. It provided a central fortified site that could serve as a centre of religious or secular power in times of peace, and could defend the people who built or maintained it in time of war. While we know a lot about these Celtic forts, we know much less about the strongholds that were used by the same people after the Romans left Britain in the early 5th century AD. The evidence they left behind us is both sparse and confusing. This is especially the case in what is now Scotland, where we know far too little about the forts which still dot the landscape.

This book takes a look at all these peoples, but our main focus is on the strongholds they built, and the role these forts played in the struggle between Pict, Scot, Briton and Angle. In these pages we'll examine the handful of known Pictish strongholds, but we'll also look at the defences built by their neighbours. We can also take a look at those forts of which very little is known – the post-Iron Age hill forts built by a Celtic people whom some scholars have dubbed the 'proto-Picts'.

This raises another couple of questions – ones that have intrigued historians and archaeologists for generations. Who exactly *were* the Picts, and why were the Scots incomers so successful in establishing themselves in Scotland?

The Picts

The Picts left behind no written history, save for the enigmatic symbols they carved on their symbol stones. Instead, apart from their archaeological footprint, what we know about them comes from outsiders – particularly

The Aberlemno Stone almost certainly commemorates the Pictish victory over the Northumbrians at the battle of Dunnichen (or Nechtansmere), fought a few kilometres from Aberlemno in AD 685. This 'Class II' Pictish stone depicts Pictish spearmen and cavalry in action.

from annalists in Northumbria or Ireland. While archaeologists still argue over the meaning of the Pictish symbol stones, their location tells us that the Picts lived on the eastern seaboard of Scotland, from Orkney and Shetland to the mainland, then down through the Highlands to the Great Glen, where Inverness stands today. Then, if one were to draw a line on the map from Inverness to Stirling at the head of the Firth of Forth, everything to the east of that line was Pictish. The greatest concentration of symbol stones is found in Moray, Aberdeenshire, Angus, Perth & Kinross and Fife.

The Picts are first mentioned by the Roman writer Eumenius in AD 297, more than a century before the Romans left Britain. The word Pict (*Picti*) was most probably a reference to 'painted people', 'people of the designs' – a reference to their supposed habit of tattooing or painting their faces or bodies. The name is clearly an all-embracing one, covering several North British tribes.

The map produced by the Alexandrian geographer Ptolemy around AD 150 provides a little more information. In Ptolemy's map seven tribes are listed in the Pictish heartland: the Venicones, Taezali, Vacomagi, Decentae, Lugi, Smertae and Cornavii, while the Caledonii occupied the central Highlands. On the west coast lay the Caereni, the Carnonacae, the Creones and the Epidii. Evidently, all these tribes were presumably embraced by the term *Picti*, including the Caledonii, which is sometimes seen as an all-encompassing name, covering the precursors of the Early Historic Picts.

In later Roman accounts the names changed – by the early 3rd century AD they were known as the Caledonii and the Maeatae, then the Caledonii and the Picti. In the mid-4th century AD these Picti were further sub-divided into the Verturiones and the Dicalydones. Whatever they were called, it seems that our Early Historic Picts were the descendants of these earlier Iron Age tribes who lived beyond the northern borders of Roman Britain. Forts dotted their territory. While most of these were the crumbling remains of old Celtic hill forts, or small fortified strongholds such as the duns, ring forts and brochs that had served the locals well for almost a millennium, others were new strongholds – centres of Pictish power, and sites which guaranteed control of their hinterland. In the coming centuries, these forts would face the onslaught of Scots, Anglo-Saxons and Vikings. The fate of these strongholds would be inextricably linked to that of the Pictish kingdom they were built to protect.

A comparison between six strongholds of the Early Historic period in Scotland, showing the marked difference in size between Burghead, Dumbarton Rock and four smaller but important Pictish or Dal Riatan fortresses (after Alcock).

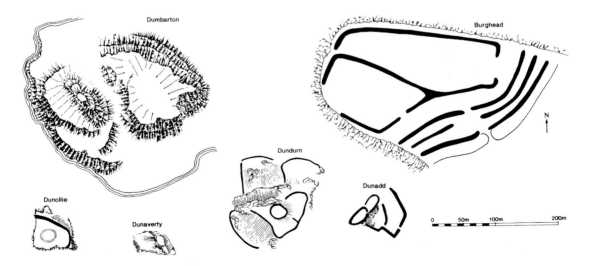

A reconstruction of the Dal Riatan dun at Kildonan in Argyll, as it might have looked in the 7th or 8th centuries AD. This was more of a fortified homestead than an important stronghold, and was typical of dozens of such structures that dotted the landscape of Scotland.

The Scots of Dal Riata

The word Scot is another example of historical shorthand. Its possible derivation is from the Latin *Scot(t)i*, which probably meant 'sea raiders'. By the mid-4th century AD the Scoti were mentioned alongside the Picts, and were described as barbarian allies who harassed the coastline of Roman Britain. In the Early Historic period the term Scot is used to describe the Dal Riata, a people who had their origins in Ireland, and who controlled parts of the west coast of Scotland.

Irish legend (recorded in the *Annals of Tigernach*) has it that the Dal Riatan kingdom was first founded in AD 500 by Fergus Mór mac Eirc, a chieftain who sought a new land for his followers, safe from the dynastic strife that plagued Ireland. It has recently been argued that political, economic and social links had spanned the short sea passage between the north of Ireland and the west of Scotland since the Bronze Age. Consequently the establishment of a Dal Riatan kingdom was less of an invasion than a confirmation of the existing political order.

By the 7th century AD the historical records show that there was a high king of Dal Riata, but his people were divided into two groups – the Cenél Loairn in the north, and the Cenél nGabráin who inhabited Kintyre in the south. The main stronghold of the Cenél Loairn was at Dunollie, just outside Oban, while the Cenél nGabráin seat was Dunadd, the imposing fortress just to the north of Kintyre which the Irish annals tell us also served as the royal seat of the high king of Dal Riata. From the mid-7th century AD these Dal Riatan Scots would become embroiled in an intermittent war with the Picts. At stake was the domination of all of Scotland north of the Forth and Clyde. The cornerstones of victory would be the Pictish and Dal Riatan strongholds that blocked access to the rival heartlands and served as centres of power.

The post-Roman Britons of southern Scotland

The Ptolemy map of *c*. AD 150 listed four tribes living between the Forth–Clyde line and Hadrian's Wall. The Votadani lived in what is now the Lothians, with their capital at Dun Eidin (Edinburgh). They were later referred to in Celtic annals and poetry as the Goddodin. They were also associated with the earlier

7

Early Historic Scotland *c.* AD 500–800

Fort
Large fort
Palace

0   50 miles

0   100km

N

Shetland

Brough of Birsay
Orkney

NORTH

SEA

Outer
Hebrides

Skye

Moray Firth

Portknockie
Burghead

Craig Phadrig

Urquhart

Loch Ness

Dunnottar

Dunollie

Inchtuthil
Inveralmond (Bertha)
Dundurn   Forteviot   Clatchard Craig
Moncreiffe
Hill

Dunadd   Stirling   Dun Eidin   Firth of Forth
                (Edinburgh)

Tarbert   Dumbarton   Dunbar
                Dalmahoy   St Abb's Head
                    Traprain
                    Law

Firth of Clyde

Dunaverty

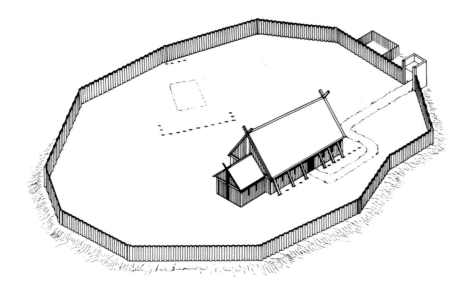

Celtic hill fort of Traprain Law. The Selgovae (a name which may mean 'hunters') occupied the land to the south, as far as the river Tweed.

On the western side of lowland Scotland the Damnonii were based along the Firth of Clyde, with their lands extending southwards from it. The Romans also gave the name to Celtic tribes in south-west England and Brittany, and it may have been a reference to either fishermen or mine-workers. These people later evolved into the Britons of Strathclyde, whose stronghold of Alt Clut – Dumbarton Rock – dominated the mouth of the river Clyde. Further to the south the Novantae (meaning 'vigorous people') occupied what is now Dumfries and Galloway. These soon became part of the British kingdom of Rheged, the territory of which spanned Hadrian's Wall.

Beyond them to the south lay other British tribes – the Carvetii, the Brigantes and the Parisi. While the Carvetii became part of the kingdom of Rheged, those further to the east fell prey to a newcomer – the Angles. During the 5th century AD these tribes formed the kingdoms of Deur and Berneich, but by the 6th century AD these had become Deira and Bernicia – part of the Anglo-Saxon kingdom of Northumbria. For the next century the Northumbrians would attempt to push their borders northwards, while the remaining British kingdoms would find themselves caught between this growing southern power and the Picts and Scots to the north. It was an unenviable position.

CHRONOLOGY

Italicized entries refer to details of Early Historic rulers, found in the *Annals of Ulster*.

297	The *Picti* are first mentioned by the Roman writer Eumenius.
367	Picts and Scots overrun Hadrian's Wall.
c.480	St Ninian leads mission to convert the southern Picts.
555–84	*Bridei, son of Mailchon is king of the Picts.*
563–97	St Columba leads mission to convert the northern Picts.
595–615	*Nechtan, son of Irb is king of the Picts.*

627	King Edwin of Northumbria (r. 617–33) is baptized.
664	Synod of Whitby leads to a split between the Roman and Celtic Church.
672	Pictish army defeated by King Ecgfrith of the Northumbrians.
673–94	*Bridei, son of Bili is king of the Picts.*
679–704	Adomnan, abbot of Iona writes his *Life of St Columba*.
681	Pictish strongholds of Dunnottar and Dundurn are besieged.
683	Dundurn is besieged and captured by Dal Riatan Scots.
685	Battle of Nechtansmere – Picts defeat the Northumbrians.
c.700	The creation of the Lindisfarne Gospel.
701	Dunollie is destroyed during civil war in Dal Riata.
c.709–24	*Nechtan, son of Derelei is king of the Picts.*
710	Ceolfrith of Jarrow requests help from Nechatan.
712	Destruction of the Scottish fort of 'Tairpert Boitter'.
728	Internecine Pictish battle fought beneath Monid Craebe (Moncreiffe Hill).
724–61	*Angus I, son of Fergus is king of the Picts.*
734	Dal Riatan stronghold of Dun Leithfinn is captured and destroyed by Picts.
736	Picts capture Dunadd during a campaign against the Dal Riatan Scots.
c.740	Foundation of church at St Andrews.
780	Strathclyde fortress of Dumbarton is destroyed by Dal Riatan Scots.
790–825	*Constantine, son of Fergus is king of the Picts.*
793–95	First Viking raids on Iona and Lindisfarne.
c.800	The Vikings conquer Orkney and Shetland.
c.820	Viking rule extended into Caithness.
c.811–20	Constantine becomes the joint king of the Picts and Scots.
c.820	The Dupplin Cross erected, and dedicated to King Constantine.
825–37	*Angus II, son of Fergus is king of Picts and Scots.*
839	Major Viking victory over the Picts.
c.843–58	*Kenneth, son of Alpin is king of Picts and Scots.*
	Note: His accession is usually seen as the foundation of a Scottish kingdom

THE EARLY HISTORIC FORTS OF SCOTLAND

Like most areas of the Early Historical period, the development of the strongholds used by the Picts, Dal Riatan Scots and their post-Roman British neighbours is a somewhat grey area. While their remains still stand, they present us with a confusing picture, although in recent decades archaeologists have done their best to unravel their mysteries. To confuse matters, several important sites show evidence of being used in more than one period – for instance in both the Iron Age and the Early Historical era. Conflicting theories have been proposed, and while the caucus of archaeological evidence has increased, many hypotheses remain unconfirmed and important questions remain unanswered.

The Scottish countryside is littered with fortified sites – in some areas it seems as if every hilltop is crowned by a fort of some kind. While most of these date from the Iron Age, several have associations with the Early Historic period, either through a handful of artefacts found there, or through the historical records. What pushed the boundaries of knowledge forward was the partial excavation of several key sites across Scotland. When this evidence is compared to information from other sites, and compared to the scant fragments of historical records, then we can begin to build up a picture of what these fortresses looked like, how they developed, and how they were used.

For the most part, the forts associated with the Early Historic period in Scotland can be divided into four main groups:

Fortified homesteads: brochs and ring forts

In northern Scotland, particularly in Orkney and Caithness, these took the form of brochs – circular stone towers, which either stood alone, or more commonly were associated with a small settlement. While these were first built in the Iron Age, there is evidence that some were still occupied during the Early Historic period. For instance, the Broch of Gurness in Orkney was used by the Picts, although there is evidence that these later dwellers allowed the broch itself to fall into disrepair, and lived in the dwelling houses clustered around it. However, the main broch period was between 600 BC and AD 100 – well before the start of our Pictish age. These structures were fortified dwelling houses serving a household or village rather than fortifications designed to protect a larger community. In this respect the broch is similar to another type of fort found further to the south in Scotland – the ring fort, or dun.

Essentially, the terms ring fort and dun refer to the same type of structure though the term 'dun' – an Irish word meaning fort – is more often used to describe the ring forts found on the western side of Scotland, or in Ireland, where they are also found in significant numbers. The word 'dun' is reflected in modern Scottish place names, such as Dunkeld, Dunblane or Dundee. It was once argued that a 'dun' was a larger and more prestigious structure than a ring fort, but now the two words are regarded as being synonymous.

The fortifications themselves are difficult to date. Most are generally assumed to date from the late Iron Age. At least one prominent archaeologist has argued that the majority of duns in the west of Scotland date from the first millennium AD, as do several ploughed-out earthen ring forts in eastern Scotland. He argues that the stone-built ring forts found in Tayside are from a later period, and therefore post-date the age of the Picts. It has been claimed that four-fifths of them were occupied from the mid-5th to the mid-9th centuries AD, and that over two-thirds of them show signs of having been rebuilt after AD 500. It is those forts lying in eastern Scotland that pose more of a problem, due to a lack of clear dating evidence.

A few of these eastern ring forts are found in the midst of complex multi-phase sites, where they are usually set in the middle of an earlier defensive structure. The builders probably wanted to take advantage of both the good defensive position and the plentiful supply of building material.

In one case – on Turin Hill near Forfar, in what would become the Pictish heartland – a ring fort was built in the middle of two earlier defensive enclosures – an Iron Age hill fort, and a smaller earthwork, which was built in the south-west corner of the larger and presumably earlier fort. The ring fort lay on one side of this smaller earthwork, so the whole assemblage of ramparts resembled a series of Russian dolls, one sitting inside another.

This suggests that the three elements represent three distinct phases of occupation, and that the ring fort was built long after the other two fell into disuse. Archaeologists dub sites of this kind 'multi-phase forts', because they were occupied over different historical periods. In some cases, the various layers of defensive works overlap each other, which clearly demonstrates the fact that the fort was reused and remodelled over the centuries. While dating sites of this kind is difficult, the evidence provided by other larger forts suggests that the Picts used stone to build their ring forts from at least the 7th century AD onwards.

The discovery of Early Historic artefacts in some of these structures suggests that a handful of ring forts were certainly used as fortified homesteads or settlements during the Pictish or Dal Riatan Scots period. However, like the brochs of Northern Scotland, they should be regarded as small, essentially domestic strongholds, rather than the more substantial Early Historic fortifications this study intends to concentrate on.

Reoccupied hill forts

Before the coming of the Romans to Britain the hill fort played a key role in the society of Celtic Scotland. The evidence then suggests that at least south of the line of Roman occupation in Scotland the forts were abandoned, or at least reduced to little more than places with a symbolic, religious significance. Strangely, the same might also have been true beyond the Roman frontier, where it appears that the majority of hill forts were abandoned until at least the 2nd or 3rd centuries AD. This might reflect the threat posed by Roman invasion or punitive expeditions launched into the lands of the Caledonii, where it was safer to avoid concentrating political and military strength in defensive sites that the Romans could capture with relative ease.

After the Romans left, fortifications became important again, although this time the strongholds were smaller. The political units of Early Historical Scotland were probably also smaller than the old tribal structures that had existed in Celtic Scotland. This meant that the old hill forts were for the most part too big to be reused, at least in their old form. However, there is evidence that some were reoccupied, thereby creating yet more 'multi-phase sites' to intrigue the archaeologists. For instance, Craig Phadrig outside Inverness, or Clatchard Craig near Newburgh in Fife, were both Iron Age hill

In this detail from General Roy's late 18th-century map of Perthshire the outlines of the Roman legionary fortress of Inchtuthil are clearly visible. The fort stood on a natural plateau, and in its south-western corner a small Early Historic fort was built, presumably by a Pictish warlord.

forts that were reoccupied by the Picts. As the majority of Iron Age hill forts in Scotland were located in the south and east, this meant that few were in the area occupied by the Dal Riatan Scots. Instead these derelict hill forts were dotted throughout the lands occupied by the Picts and the post-Roman Britons in what is now southern Scotland.

In 1988 Professor Leslie Alcock argued that these hill forts could be divided into two main groups. The first of these were the classic multivallate Celtic hill forts, with several banks and ditches surrounding an inner sanctum. These were almost always built on conspicuous hills, as at Traprain Law, Clatchard Craig and Craig Phadrig. His second group – the univallate fort – tended to be found near the sea, on a promontory. These were usually associated with timber palisade defences, such as those at Dumbarton Rock or Portknockie. A multivallate version of this kind of fort is found at Burghead, which combines a position on a promontory with multivallate defences and timber-laced ramparts. In addition to these two main groups, Alcock includes an extra category – the palisade fort. This is a more basic type of fortification consisting of a simple wooden palisade, and was probably used to protect important, timber-built, secular buildings. This type of fortification is found at Portknockie or in the earliest defensive works at Dundurn.

A few of these multivallate hill forts are worth looking at in a little more detail. For instance, Craig Phadrig on the eastern outskirts of Inverness was an important strronghold in the 6th and 7th centuries AD. This site consisted of an Iron Age hill fort whose stone defences were vitrified. This occurs when the timbers used to form a framework for the stone wall are set alight. The heat melts the stones, thereby creating vitrification. While the builders may have done this deliberately, it seems more likely that it took place when the fort was captured, and the timbers set alight. The fort was then reoccupied during the Early Historic period, and pottery finds, which were produced in France during the 7th century AD, suggest that it was a site of some considerable importance.

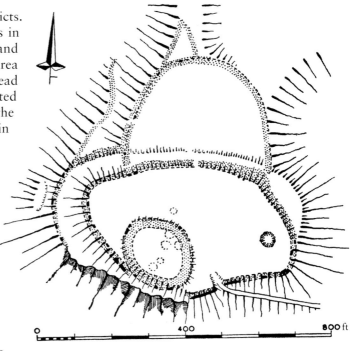

A plan of Moncreiffe Hill near Perth, a major Pictish stronghold. The site was in use during the Iron Age, but after the departure of the Romans it was rebuilt as an Early Historic hill fort, with timber-laced, stone-built walls built on top of the earlier ramparts. A ring fort citadel formed the core of the hill's defences.

The Romans abandoned the fort at Inchtuthil in the late 1st century AD, but the site was later reoccupied and a small Pictish or proto-Pictish fort was built in the open area seen here, immediately to the south-west of the Roman ramparts.

It may even have been the seat of King Bridei, son of Mailchon (r. AD 558–84), who received a mission from St Columba that had travelled up the Great Glen to the Pictish king's stronghold from Iona. As Adomnan recorded in his *Life of St Columba*, 'the first time St Columba climbed the steep path to King Bridei's fortress, the king – swollen with royal dignity – acted haughtily, and at first refused to open the gates of his fortress when the blessed man appeared'. Some scholars have argued that the site of this important meeting took place at Urquhart on the shores of Loch Ness, where a small fortress pre-dated the medieval castle that now stands on the same site. However, the description of the steep climb is better suited to Craig Phadrig.

The fort is not a particularly large one. The interior occupies an area of approximately 240 square metres (2,500 square feet), surrounded by an earthen bank. This was surmounted by an impressive stone wall, standing nearly four metres (13ft) high on its outward face, and one metre (three feet) on the level of the interior of the fort. Outside this oval-shaped inner defence lies a ditch and an outer bank. Beyond this the hill drops off sharply on all sides, which accentuates the defensive qualities of the stronghold. The wall itself was once timber faced, and was subsequently vitrified. The earliest date for a fort on the site was the 4th century BC, based on radiocarbon evidence. In the interior of the fort the earlier levels were covered by what archaeologists call a sterile layer – evidence that the fort fell into disuse during the later Iron Age.

Finds from layers above this have been attributed to the Pictish period, and suggest a period of later occupancy during the 4th to the 6th centuries AD. Excavation has revealed that the older vitrified ramparts were partially rebuilt during this period, although evidence for this is sparse. The relative importance of the finds from the Early Historic period suggest that even if Craig Phadrig wasn't the late 6th-century stronghold of King Bridei of the Picts, then it was certainly an important fortified site during his reign.

A similar Iron Age hill fort on Clatchard Craig in Fife was also rebuilt during the Pictish period. It stood on the top of a steep rocky crag overlooking the Tay Estuary, near the modern town of Newburgh. One side of the fort lay at the edge of a cliff face, so the site only needed to be defended on its remaining sides, which made it slightly different from the classic hill forts found elsewhere. Unfortunately the hill fort was destroyed by quarrying during the mid 20th century, but not before the site was extensively excavated. This revealed that this was very much a multi-phase site, as fragments of both Neolithic and Iron Age pottery were found, as well as finds from the Early Historic period. This was a multivallate hill fort, with no fewer than six banks or ramparts enclosing its landward perimeter. The innermost bank encircled an oval-shaped hilltop on the edge of the cliff, forming the inner enclosure of the fort. It appears that this rampart was a substantial, stone-built affair. It was timber laced, and had been burnt at some stage, causing vitrification. Radiocarbon dating places its construction at some time during the 5th or early 6th centuries AD.

Another rampart surrounding the lower slopes of the hill dates from the same period. These were then extensively rebuilt around AD 600, at which point three outer ramparts were added on the lower slopes of the hill. The first of these fully encircles the innermost ramparts, running around the hill to the edges of the cliff. Beyond it, two more ramparts protect this circuit of defences, and were probably also designed to encircle the fort, though traces of their central portions have since been lost to agriculture. Taken together, these five sets of banks and ramparts would have created an extremely imposing defensive work.

So far the development of the site is simple enough – a smallish fort, built on the site of an earlier Iron Age hill fort, is damaged by fire around AD 600, at which point it is rebuilt and turned into a much larger and far more imposing 7th-century Pictish stronghold. However, a feature labelled 'Rampart 2' messes up the otherwise neat chronology. While the other ramparts conform to the natural contours of the hill, Rampart 2 cuts across them. It was built as an extension to the innermost rampart, and encircles a relatively flat area of lower terrace within the perimeter of the next 7th-century rampart. In effect it resembles the bailey of a Norman motte and bailey castle. It may have built as a deliberate attempt to shorten the circuit of the defensive perimeter, while still enclosing a substantial inner area, suitable for the storage of livestock, the construction of buildings, or the housing of stores.

Roman masonry was used in its construction, presumably transported to the site from the fort at Carpow a short distance to the west. This means that this phase of the construction clearly postdates the departure of the Romans from Britain. In fact this inner feature has been dated to the 8th or early 9th century AD, the very end of the Pictish period. This means that the fort may well have been abandoned during the Pictish period, then reoccupied and refortified, albeit on a less imposing scale. What this demonstrates is that when it comes to Early Historic fortifications, nothing is quite what it seems, and only the most painstaking archaeology can help us understand how and when these forts were used.

Promontory forts

Promontory forts were built close to the sea to take advantage of the natural defences offered by the coast. Most of these were simple, univallate affairs with timber defences, such as the Mote of Mark in Dumfries and Galloway, in the south-west of Scotland, and Dumbarton Rock, the seat of the Britons of Strathclyde, which stands sentinel over the estuary of the river Clyde. In the north-east of Scotland lies Green Castle, a small promontory fort just

The Mote of Mark is a small hilltop fort overlooking the estuary of the river Urr, in Dumfries and Galloway. The site was occupied during the 6th century AD, and it has been suggested that it formed the stronghold of a sub-king of the British kingdom of Rheged.

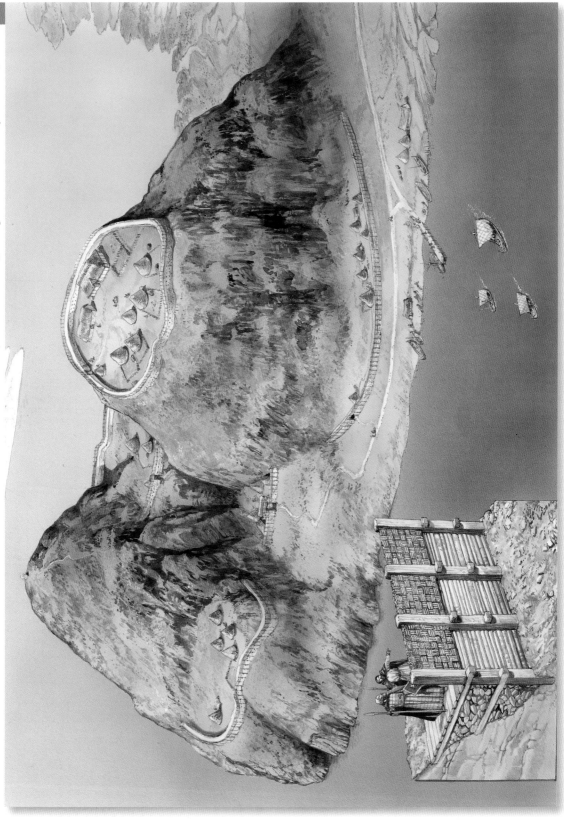

Alt Clut (Dumbarton Rock), stronghold of the Strathclyde Britons, AD 870

A

The name Alt Clut or Alcuith (meaning Rock of the Clyde) was mentioned by Bede (AD 672–735), and he was almost certainly referring to the stronghold built on Dumbarton Rock, a volcanic plug that looms over the upper reaches of the Firth of Clyde. It was occupied during the Iron Age, but from the 5th century AD the rock served as the fortified capital of the kingdom of Strathclyde, an independent post-Roman British state. It remained an important regional stronghold until AD 870, when Alt Clut was besieged, captured and sacked by a Norse (Viking) army, led by kings Olaf and Ivar, of Dublin. According

to Norse annals, the treasure and slaves looted from the fortress filled 200 Norse longships.

This reconstruction of the fortress shows it as it might have looked in the 8th or early 9th centuries AD, before the Norse siege. Although the archaeological evidence is scanty, the rock was defended on its one landward side by a wooden palisade, while further fortifications most probably covered the approaches to the summit, where a central stone-built citadel would most probably have been located. While this reconstruction is conjectural, the inset shows the palisade wall, based on solid archaeological evidence.

outside Portknockie on the Moray Firth, while the largest promontory fort of them all lies a few kilometres away at Burghead, which was a major stronghold defended by a complex multivallate system of ramparts, walls and ditches. It could even be argued that the Early Historic fort that lies beneath Urquhart Castle, on the shores of Loch Ness was another univallate promontory fort, albeit on the side of a loch rather than the sea.

The Mote of Mark stands above the village of Rockcliffe, overlooking the estuary of the river Urr where it empties into the Solway Firth. The small hill fort was excavated in 1913, and again in 1973, and it was discovered that a large circular hall surrounded by a timber-laced wooden rampart once crowned its tiny summit. Vitrification took place at some time, possibly during a siege by the Angles, as their inscriptions have been found within the walls. It was initially thought that these defences were built during the 9th century AD, but the later excavations suggested a much earlier date during the 6th or 7th centuries AD.

Dunnottar Castle near Stonehaven, viewed through the North Sea haar (mist). This natural stronghold was only accessible by means of a steep track, where the path leads today. The archaeological evidence suggests that the summit was protected by a bank and rampart, beneath where the hall of the medieval castle now stands.

Dumbarton Rock was the *Civitas Brettonum munitissima* (political centre of the Britons) of Bede's *The Ecclesiastical History of the English People* (AD 731). Of all the Early Historic strongholds in Scotland, Dumbarton – or Alt Clut as Bede called it – has the greatest number of historical references available to back up the scant archaeological evidence. For instance, we know the stronghold was captured and destroyed by the Norse raiders Olaf and Ivar the Boneless in AD 870. Bede mentions the fort in his *History*, suggesting it might have been an important site long before the venerable cleric wrote about it. One of the early occupants of Alt Clut might have been the warlord Coroticus, whom St Patrick wrote to in the late 7th century AD. In his *Life of St Columba*, Abbot Adomnan of Iona mentions a Rodericus, son of Tothal, whose seat was the Rock of the Clyde. This could only mean Dumbarton.

Excavations on the site in 1974/75 revealed evidence of a timber-fronted rubble and earth rampart, sited at the base of the rock on its eastern side. This is where a spur of land linked the rock to the mainland. It appears that the base of this rampart was about 2.5m (eight feet) wide, and another two metres (seven feet) high. The wooden or wicker palisade would have run along the top of this substantial rampart. Radiocarbon dating places its construction at some time during the 6th or early 7th centuries AD. It seems unlikely that this rampart encircled the whole rock, it probably only protected its landward approaches. The steepness of the rock, combined with its proximity to the river Clyde, would have made more extensive defences unnecessary. Instead it is assumed that the rampart stretched between two impenetrable crags that formed either end of the eastern face of the rock.

Unfortunately, later defences on the site have obliterated all other traces of this 7th-century stronghold. The remains of stone walls that were once thought to date to the Early Historic period were subsequently found to date from the 13th century. Therefore it seems that, despite its formidable natural defences, this timber palisade and rubble rampart formed the main line of defence at Alt Clut. As the landward approach to the rock was covered by water at low tide during this period, these simple defences were both effective and economical. However, they failed to deter the Norsemen, who captured Alt Clut in the late 9th century AD. Evidence of vitrification in the rubble of the rampart suggests that the defences were destroyed, and one can infer that this took place when the fort was captured in AD 870.

The small Dal Riatan Scots' stronghold of Dunollie stands beside the modern entrance into Oban Harbour. In the Early Historic period a ring fort stood where the medieval castle now stands, protected by stone-built outworks on its landward side.

Of the other smaller promontory forts, both Urquhart and Dunnottar became the site of medieval castles and so little trace remains of the Early Historic defences. The *Annals of Ulster* suggest that Dunnottar (then called Dun Fother) was a Pictish stronghold that was besieged – presumably by the Dal Riatan Scots – in AD 681, and then besieged again in AD 694. According to the *Chronicle of the Kings of Alba* it was finally captured and destroyed by the Norsemen during the reign of the Pictish king Donald, son of Constantine, around AD 900. The location is ideal. It lies on the coast at the point where the Mounth, the eastern range of the Grampian Mountains, comes within a few kilometres of the North Sea. This effectively creates a strategic bottleneck, and makes Dunnottar an ideal place to site a fortress. It has also been suggested that the Mounth separated the northern and southern portions of the Pictish kingdom, which placed Dunnottar – or Dun Fother – on the border.

Dunnottar Castle stands on the flat summit of a small rocky promontory, whose steep sides make it inaccessible from the sea. On the landward side a narrow spine-like causeway provides a link between the crag and the mainland. Excavations at Dunnottar were carried out during the late 1970s, and then again in 1984. Traces of an early defensive bank were discovered beneath the walls of the medieval castle, sited to cover the approach to the crag via the causeway. However, traces were also found of another earthwork on the cliff top overlooking the causeway. This might well have formed part of an outwork, or – as at Tintagel in Cornwall – it may have been the main site of the stronghold, with the craggy promontory beyond affording only the most basic of defences. More archaeological work needs to be carried out here to work out exactly where Dun Fother was located.

At Urquhart, on the western shore of Loch Ness, an excavation in 1983 revealed possible traces of a stone-built citadel. Although radiocarbon evidence was imprecise, this may well have been built during the Early Historic period. Vitrified stone was found at the base of the small mound on which the central keep of the medieval castle had been built, and the excavation suggested that this might have formed part of a timber-laced stone wall. It was also surmised that traces of another smaller dry-stone wall might once have formed part of a wall encircling the flat terrace beneath the citadel, forming a first line of defence on the landward side of the stronghold. Of course, due to the medieval castle, many of these theories will never be tested through a more thorough excavation. The historical sources are also confusing. While Urquhart may have been the site of the meeting between St Columba and the Pictish king Bridei in the late 6th century AD, Cairn Phadrig near Inverness remains a stronger contender. According to Abbot Adomnan, the meeting took place in the king's great hall (*aula regia*), so either of the two strongholds would have formed the seat of Pictish power during this period.

Several other coastal sites boast fortifications from this period, including Dunaverty in Kintyre, Dunbar and St Abb's Head in south-east Scotland, and Dunollie in the heart of Dal Riata. However, some of the most spectacular promontory forts lie in north-east Scotland, in what was once the territory of the northern Picts. These range from the small strongholds of Castle Point (or Cullykhan) near Pennan, and Green Castle, Portknockie, 32km (20 miles) to the west, to the far more impressive stronghold of Burghead, another 48km (30 miles) to the west of Portknockie. Other similar but undated sites on the same coast also include Cleaved Head, Macduff, which lies midway between Pennan and Portknockie and which now forms part of a golf course; Crathie Pot, Sandend, just a few kilometres east of Portknockie; and Dundarg, the site

Portknockie, Pictish promontory fort, c. AD 780

of a ruined castle a few kilometres west of Pennan. All these promontory forts overlook the Moray Firth.

The small promontory fort of 'Green Castle' is typical of these smaller sites. It forms a small 20m-high (66ft) rocky outcrop that shelters the small harbour at Portknockie from the sea. The uneven summit of the outcrop covers an area approximately 70m (230ft) long, and 15m (50ft) wide. While few traces of the defences can be seen, apart from an eroded low bank on the south-west corner of the plateau, excavation has indicated that the site was occupied during the Iron Age, when a palisade was built to protect the plateau on its landward side. In the Early Historic period, the fort was rebuilt, this time with a more elaborate timber-laced stone rampart surrounding a hall, which stood in the centre of the small plateau. The defences were destroyed by fire at some point, possibly during an attack by Norse raiders. Radiocarbon dating suggests these substantial ramparts were constructed during the 7th and late 8th centuries AD – a period whose end marks the commencement of Norse raids on the northern Pictish kingdom. It is therefore not too far-fetched to suggest that this small fort was refortified as a means of countering the Norse threat.

A similar story is provided by the archaeological evidence from the far more substantial promontory fort at Burghead. This great promontory fort was a multivallate site, with no fewer than three ramparts sealing off the base of a promontory on its landward side. The original defences might well have been constructed during the Iron Age, but these were extensively rebuilt

This shows the interior of the small Pictish promontory fort at Portknockie, on the coast of the Moray Firth. Archaeological evidence suggests that a hall stood here, protected by a stone-built rampart. Unfortunately little visible trace remains of this Pictish bastion against the Norsemen.

B PORTKNOCKIE, PICTISH PROMONTORY FORT, c. AD 780

Not all promontory forts were large, or even heavily fortified on their landward side. The small fort at Portknockie on the coast of the Moray Firth was built on a small rock outcrop, barely 70m (230ft) long, and 15m (50ft) wide, bounded by steep cliffs. Known locally as 'Green Castle', it was sealed off from the land by means of a timber-laced stone wall, the traces of which are now almost non-existent. The site was excavated during the 1970s, and this revealed the presence of stone buildings on the top of the plateau and timber-laced stone defences protecting the southern side of the fort.

Dating evidence suggests that this small fort was built during the 7th or 8th centuries AD, possibly in response to the threat of Norse raids. It also seems to have been damaged by fire, which suggests that it was besieged and destroyed – most probably by the same Norsemen whose raids led to its construction in the first place. Today 'Green Castle' protects the small harbour of Portknockie from the sea. It has been suggested that the fort was built there to protect a Pictish harbour, which might have been anything from a fishing haven to a base for Pictish raiding craft. This reconstruction is based on the limited archaeological evidence, but it demonstrates how the Picts made good use of the natural defensive qualities of the rock, and the 20m-high (66ft) cliffs that surround it.

during the Early Historic period. Even as late as the 18th century, Burghead must have been one of the most impressive ancient fortified sites in Scotland. However, most of these defences were levelled during the early 19th century when its stones were used for the rebuilding of Burghead harbour, and a neatly planned new village was built over the remains.

Fortunately the military cartographer General William Roy (1726–90) produced a detailed plan of the old defences that was published in 1793, three years after his death. This shows that the original fort was divided into two sections, divided by a substantial rampart, the traces of which can still be seen today. The higher section to the west probably formed a royal enclosure containing a royal hall and dwelling, while the slightly larger eastern enclosure may well have housed a settlement. A large well built during the Early Historic period still survives and, according to Roy's plan, would have stood near the outer wall of this northern enclosure.

The ramparts themselves would have been over six metres (20ft) high, and seven to eight metres (23–28ft) thick. A solid sandstone revetment formed the inner and outer faces, while the space between was framed with timber lacing and then filled with stone rubble. Archaeological evidence suggests that this timber framework of squared oak beams was actually nailed together to form a grid, while the beams set at right angles to the wall almost certainly protruded slightly from it. Radiocarbon dating has shown that these walls were first constructed before the departure of the Romans from Britain, possibly as early as the late 3rd century AD. Other dating evidence suggests that the walls were refurbished later in the Pictish period, during the 6th or 7th centuries AD.

An unusual feature of this multivallate promontory fort was that its design – with three lines of earthen ramparts preceding the main inner rampart – was typical of the Celtic forts built in France and Britain during the late Iron Age. The inference is that the Picts simply reoccupied an older Iron Age stronghold and made its already impressive defences even more formidable by adding the timber-laced stone wall. If the radiocarbon dates are correct, Burghead may well have been an important regional stronghold for the best part of five centuries. This importance is reflected in the archaeological finds recovered from the site, including a number of stones decorated with Pictish carvings. The most common image on these stones is a bull, and similar bull carvings were found on six stones recovered during repairs to Burghead's quayside or houses. This suggests that they came from the stonework of the main rampart, and it has even been suggested that these might have once have been used to decorate the entranceway or outer wall of the stronghold.

Other decorated stones found in the new town's churchyard, dating from around AD 800, probably once formed part of Christian crosses, suggesting that Burghead was a centre of religious as well as secular significance by the end of the Pictish period. Repairs to the wall can also be dated to this period, when the threat posed by Norse raiders was at its height. According to the *Annals of Ulster* of AD 839: 'The heathens [Norsemen] won a battle against the men of Fortriu [the northern Picts], and Eóganán son of Aengus, Bran son of Óengus, Aed son of Boanta, and others almost innumerable fell there.' The entry in the *Annals* concluded by claiming that in the aftermath of this defeat 'the foreigners burnt Ferna and Corcach'. The location of these two sites is unknown, but one may have been an old name for Burghead, a name which is Norse rather than Pictish in origin. This burning coincided with the end of any sign of occupancy at Burghead. It all suggests that this great Pictish stronghold finally succumbed to the Viking invaders.

The Pictish promontory fort at Burghead is divided by a high bank, with one portion being higher than the other. This view of the site shows the larger, lower enclosure of the fort, with the outer rampart facing the modern buildings.

The higher, smaller enclosure at Burghead, seen from the central internal wall of the fort, looking towards the south-west and the outer rampart, which starts just before the modern buildings.

The height difference between the two internal enclosures at Burghead is clearly seen in this photograph, looking towards the Moray Firth to the north. It has been suggested that the area on the left was of considerable secular or religious importance.

Dun Fother (Dunnottar), Pictish promontory fort, c. AD 700

DUN FOTHER (DUNNOTTAR), PICTISH PROMONTORY FORT, *c.* AD 700

Today an imposing medieval castle crowns the rocky peninsula at Dunnottar south of Stonehaven. The site was also occupied during the Early Historic period, and it is mentioned in the *Annals of Ulster* entries for AD 680 and 693. The *Scottish Chronicle* also mentions that it was destroyed by Norse raiders during the late 9th century AD. An archaeological investigation in 1984 suggested that the neck of the promontory on which the medieval castle now stands was fortified during this period, and this may well have formed part of the defences of Dun Fother.

However, further excavation revealed the presence of Early Historic defences on the landward side of the promontory, and

what may well have been an area of domestic buildings. This suggests that the site might have been more complex than anyone thought, with defences on both sides of the narrow causeway. To complicate matters further, just 400m (1,312ft) to the north is another headland called Dunnicaer, which now forms an isolated stack. Pictish symbol stones were found there in the 19th century, and a survey revealed that – like Dunnottar – the neck of this peninsula was sealed with a rampart during the Early Historic period. Clearly a lot more lies uncovered, but the reconstruction offered here is based on the tantalizing results of this excavation.

Citadel forts and nuclear forts

The final category of Early Historic period defences represents an amalgam of two archaeological theories. In 1948 the archaeologist Robert Stevenson produced a groundbreaking study of these forts, in which he outlined the concept of the 'nuclear' fort. R.W. Feachem reinforced his definition in 1955, when his essay on fortifications was published in F. T. Wainwright's *The Problem of the Picts*. According to Stevenson and Feachem, a 'nuclear' fort differed from other 'Dark Age' strongholds in two ways. First, the hill it stood on was elongated rather than circular, with space on its upper slopes for human habitation. Just like in other hill forts, ring forts or duns the defences took advantage of natural features to bolster their strength. However, unlike large citadel-like ring forts, these strongholds were flanked by defensive enclosures, the innermost of which extended outwards from the walls of a central stone-built citadel. Outer walls might then extend out from these secondary walls to form a complex network of defences encompassing the hilltop or crag.

Stevenson used the fort at Dalmahoy in Midlothian as an example. The fort stands on top of a steep volcanic hill between Edinburgh and Livingston, and from the remains of its ramparts an observer can see Edinburgh Castle 11km (seven miles) to the east, once the site of the Early Historic fortress of Dun Eidin, mentioned in the epic poem *Y Goddodin*. Interestingly, the fort at Dalmahoy was built next to an Iron Age fort on the adjacent Kaimes Hill. The inference was that Kaimes Hill had already been abandoned when Dalmahoy was built.

The 'nuclear' hill fort at Dalmahoy in Midlothian covers a long, narrow hill, and is divided into several small enclosures. This important regional fortress was occupied during the Early Historic period, although there is information to be gleaned about it and its occupants from contemporary historic records.

The sheer side of the north face of Dalmahoy hill fort shows just how good a naturally defensive site it was. The builders of the fortress used this terrain to their advantage, and concentrated most of their efforts on defending the site from attack from the south, where the slope was far gentler.

Dalmahoy was a 'nuclear' hill fort, with its central citadel standing on this small rocky outcrop. From there outworks looped outwards to cover the ridge to either side. The rocky hill at Dun Eidin (now Edinburgh Castle) can easily be seen 11km (seven miles) away to the east.

The fort itself consisted of an oval-shaped central citadel – essentially a large ring fort – built on the highest part of the hill. On the ridge to either side lay a series of stone-walled outer defences, designed to take advantage of the rocky crags and slopes that increased the natural defensive qualities of the site. A handful of finds from the Early Historic period suggest that the fort itself can be dated fairly approximately to the 6th or 7th centuries AD. This coincides with the northward expansion of Northumbria into what is now east central Scotland – the territory of the Goddodin. Dun Eidin fell to the Angles in AD 638, and we might assume that Dalmahoy succumbed to these invaders around the same time.

Stevenson went on to link the 'nuclear' fort of Dalmahoy with other similar Early Historic strongholds – most notably the major Pictish fort at Dundurn, and the important Scottish one at Dunadd. Feachem supported this association, although he also added another fort to the 'nuclear' family – Moncreiffe Hill near Perth (called Monid Craebe in the historic records), which he claimed was an example of a 'nuclear' fort that had been built by altering and augmenting the stone-built defences of an earlier hill fort. Interestingly, both Stevenson and Feachem emphasized the importance of a central citadel to the design of a 'nuclear' fort. However, they also insisted that 'nuclear' forts were notably different to less complex 'citadel' forts. These consisted of a large ring fort surrounded by outworks, which were not linked to the central citadel. The inference was that the 'nuclear' fort was a later development of the 'citadel' fort.

Feachem offered Dumyat in the Ochil Hills near Stirling as a prime example of a 'citadel' fort, where a large stone-built ring fort stood alone on the summit of a crag, while steep cliffs and a gully protected three sides of the hilltop around it. On its western side two stone-built outer walls protected the citadel enclosure from attack. Ferachem suggested that Dumyat was the stronghold of the Maeatae, a people who the Roman chronicler Cassius Dio (c.164–229) claimed, 'live close to the wall that divides the island into two parts'. The Antonine Wall – occupied, abandoned and reoccupied during Dio Cassius' lifetime – lay 16km (ten miles) south of the fort. Dumyat may well have been the principal fortress of the Maetae, but Feachem used this assumption to strengthen his theory that the 'citadel' fort predated the 'nuclear' fort by at least three centuries. Incidentally, he also names the Iron Age hill fort at Myot Hill as another possible Maetae stronghold, and it lies less than three kilometres (two miles) from the line of the Roman wall.

In 1988 Professor Leslie Alcock re-examined this nomenclature in the light of more than two decades of excavation, including work on both Dundurn and Dunadd. He argued that Dundurn was actually a multi-phase fort, which – in its simplest form – consisted of a crag defended by a wooden palisade. This was augmented by a simple ring fort – the 'citadel' – which in turn was protected by outworks. These were then expanded to form a 'nuclear' fort. In other words, a single fort could develop over time, and in the process could cross the boundaries between categories. He therefore proposed his own system:

Category A forts defended by a simple wooden palisade. Examples included the earliest defences at Portknockie or Dundurn.

Category B hill forts of the type in use during the Iron Age and subsequently reoccupied during the Early Historic period. Alcock divided these into two subgroups. B1 was composed of multivallate hill forts, which included Clatchard Craig, Craig Phadrig, as well as East Lomond hill fort in Fife and Tynron Doon in Dumfries and Galloway. B2 were univallate forts, usually on promontories and often with timber-framed defences. These included Dumbarton Rock, the Mote of Mark, and the later phases at Portknockie and Dundurn. He argued that although Burghead was a multivallate fort, its promontory setting meant it really belonged in this second category.

Category C forts dated to the 1st millennium AD. Alcock split these into three subgroups. C1 consisted of the simple ring forts, which included the duns of western Scotland. Examples included the earliest phases of Dunadd and Dunollie. C2 comprised ring forts with outworks, which ranged from forecourts to full-scale enclosing walls. This category includes the 'citadel' forts described by Feachem. Examples include the later stage of development at Dunollie, as well as Dumyat, Moncreiffe Hill and the King's Seat at Dunkeld. The largest forts were labelled C3. These included Stevenson's 'nuclear' forts. Alcock categorized them as having articulated, hierarchically arranged enclosures, where the plan was conceived as a single work. Examples included Dalmahoy, and the last stages of development at Dunadd and Dundurn. He also added another possible example – Ruberslaw fort in the Borders.

Alcock went on to discuss the problem of classifying C2 and C3 forts. He claimed that Feachem repudiated Stevenson's notion of a 'citadel' fort, arguing that they were probably ring forts built in the middle of earlier enclosures – a bit like the Turin Hill fort described earlier. Alcock's programme of excavation also revealed that many 'citadel' and 'nuclear' forts were multi-phase, and therefore shouldn't be classified in simplistic terms, based simply on their appearance. Besides, these forts could be misleading – excavation at Dumbarton Rock revealed that the outworks that had once been ascribed to a 'nuclear' fort were in fact medieval additions. Instead, the Early Historic forts of Scotland evolved over the centuries, and reached their high point in the impressive 'nuclear' forts of Dundurn and Dunadd.

DUNDURN AND DUNADD: A TOUR OF TWO GREAT STRONGHOLDS

Of all the forts mentioned above two strongholds stand out, both for their impressive appearance and because they represent the final evolutionary stage in the development of Early Historic fortifications in Scotland. Dundurn was a bastion of the Picts, defending the western approaches to the Pictish heartland. It has also been suggested it was a regional capital. Dunadd was almost certainly the principal seat of power in Dal Riata, the base from which

The Pictish hilltop stronghold of Dundurn, viewed from the north. The main defences began just above the modern tree line, and were concentrated on this northern side of the summit. A timber-laced, stone-built citadel once crowned the highest point of the small hill.

The summit of Dundurn, viewed from the spot where the pathway entered the lower enclosure of the fort. Bastions on the high ground to the right would have made this approach a difficult one for any attacker. The start of a second courtyard can be seen on the far left of the photograph.

All that remains of the ramparts at Dundurn are these lines of rock scree, which represent the lines of the defences. The dry-stone walling of the ramparts was either demolished deliberately, or collapsed during the intervening centuries. These stones lie immediately to the west of the first enclosure, marked 'G' on the Christison map of the fort on page 31.

the Dal Riatan Scots kings planned their expansion across the central spine of Scotland. The easiest way to describe how both of these important strongholds looked and functioned is to tour the forts, noting their similarities and differences as we go.

Dundurn

Dundurn rises out of the valley floor of Strathearn like a sentinel, blocking the way to the rich farmlands lying to the east. It stands on top of a large, crag-like hill – a natural pyramid of rock – protected by a boulder and small

The summit of Dundurn, viewed from the east. The rock scree in the foreground probably represents part of the demolished stonework of the citadel, which once crowned this small knoll. In the 7th and 8th centuries AD this lower area would have formed part of the upper courtyard of the fortress.

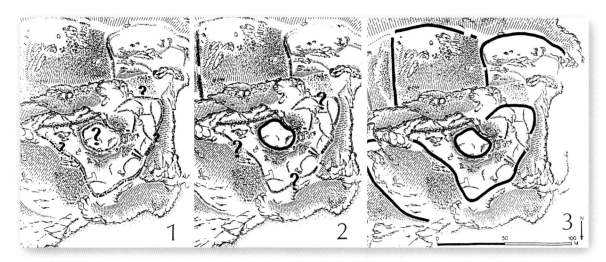

According to the late Professor Leslie Alcock, the complex defences of Dundurn developed in three main phases, although the exact details of what was built when remains unclear. The 'nuclear' fort was the final phase of construction, and probably dates from the 8th century AD.

stone scree on its lower slopes, and by sheer faces of exposed rock closer to its dome-like summit. This highest point forms a rocky oval, surrounded by lower terraces that form something of a plateau, surrounded by steep slopes and rocky precipices. The hill fort specialist A. H. A Hogg said of Dundurn that, 'From the north, its resemblance to a huge clenched left fist, palm upwards, is not entirely fanciful, and may account for the name.' *Dòrn* is the modern Gaelic word for 'fist'. This is almost certainly the site mentioned in the *Annals of Ulster*, which – like Dunadd – was besieged in AD 683.

The fort can only be approached from its western side, as sheer-faced crags protect the southern and eastern slopes, while the northern face is too sheer to climb without great difficulty. Of this western side, only the north-western quadrant is accessible, as on its south-eastern side the rocky slope is both too steep to climb, and flanked by low cliffs. In the 8th century AD, a visitor would approach the fortress by climbing the lower slopes on the north-west corner of Dundurn. Unfortunately we don't know exactly how these would have looked as they have never been more than cursorily examined by archaeologists. However, the visitor would have been faced with a stone wall, while to his right the citadel and its western outwork would have loomed over him. A defender armed with javelin, bow or crossbow could have turned this approach into a killing ground.

Some form of entranceway was set in the northern side of the rampart in front of the visitor, and once through this gateway he would have entered an enclosure. The visitor would then have followed the path which wound its way clockwise up and around the hill, passing through two more enclosures or courtyards, each overlooked by the walls of higher courtyards and the citadel on the summit. Another steeper track led straight down the south-western slope, emerging from a line of outworks that form the westernmost enclosure – a form of defensive outwork designed to cover the only accessible route into the fort.

Once he reached the summit the visitor would find himself in an uppermost courtyard or enclosure, which covered the southern side of the hill. It encompassed a triangular area approximately 100m (328ft) long on each of its three sides. Its northern rampart overlooked the lower courtyards, while its western edge faced the lower western enclosure – the one that covered the approaches to the fort. The third face of the triangle – the south-east side – was probably lined by another rampart, running along the top of the cliff-like crag. A small, crescent-shaped outwork extended beyond and below the northern

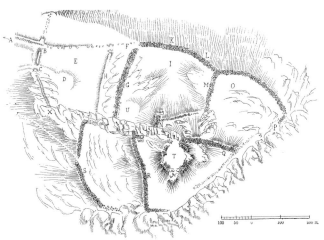

wall, as if designed to cover the main path as it wound its through the lower way up and around the hill.

A well might have been located in the north-west corner of this hilltop enclosure, which may well have been filled with buildings. Archaeologists found remains of timber and flooring here, which suggests some form of habitation. Also found were traces of a midden that contained wood chippings, cherry stones and other forms of domestic refuse. Unfortunately, most of this upper enclosure remains unexcavated, largely because the productive archaeological layers that produced organic remains were much deeper than the excavating team expected. However, we can assume that the area was used by the fortress dwellers and was habitable. Finally, dominating the whole plateau was the summit – an oval-shaped area approximately 40m (131ft) long and 20m (66ft) wide. This is where a central citadel stood.

The citadel was also oval, to match the natural rock-covered mound on which it stood. Its walls were thick and interlaced by a timber framework, which – as at Burghead – was probably fastened together using iron spikes. This would probably have been laid in a grid pattern, and then filled in with stone rubble, before the ramparts were faced with dry-stone walling. It is unclear just how high or even how thick this oval-shaped wall would have been, but the interior of the oval has been estimated at approximately 25m (82ft) by 18m (59ft). Unfortunately, a single post-hole was the only indication of an internal structure, but one would expect the citadel to have been roofed to form a great hall, or to have contained a smaller high-status structure.

ABOVE LEFT
The Pictish hilltop stronghold of Dundurn (Dun Durn), viewed from the higher hills on the southern side of Strathearn. The fortress consisted of a citadel on the summit, with outworks covering the main approaches to the top. The main approach was on the far – western – side. (RCAHMS)

ABOVE RIGHT
The 'nuclear' fort of Dundurn, as sketched by D. Christison at the start of the 20th century, used to illustrate a series of reports in the *Proceedings of the Society of Antiquaries in Scotland*. It clearly shows how the spiral nature of the defences, with a series of courtyards guarding from an attack up the main approach, as it wound its spiral way up the hill from the west (north is to the top).

LEFT
Dundurn viewed from the north-west, as sketched by Christison. It shows the slope of the main approach path, as it climbs the slope, past the first set of outworks, before entering one of the lower enclosures of the fort, on the far left. The main inhabited area lay beyond the crest, which was crowned by a citadel.

The western approaches to Dundurn, viewed from the summit. The scree line marks the site of the western rampart. Below it ran a second outer line of defence, protecting a lower shoulder of the hill, and providing a flanking position where defenders could fire missiles at attackers approaching up the main pathway.

Dundurn, viewed from the west. The approach path ran up through the trees from bottom right to top left in this photograph, until it entered a gateway into the outer courtyard of the fort on the high ground in the middle distance.

This tour of Dundurn is based on its probable appearance during the late 7th century AD. In fact the fort was refortified at least three times during the Early Historic period. The earliest fortification was a palisade that ran around the triangular upper enclosure, anchored to a wooden beam set into a trench cut into the bare rock. This has been dated with some precision to around AD 600. This wooden stockade was then either dismantled or repaired – the evidence suggests either option during which the hilltop appears to have been undefended. The dating of this phase is almost too vague to be useful, but it appears to have taken place around the mid 7th century AD.

Then, in the later 7th century AD the hilltop was refortified and the citadel was built on the highest point on the hill. This may have taken place after the siege of AD 683, which meant that at the time of the siege Dundurn was poorly defended. However, the dating evidence is vague, and the timber-laced citadel could have been standing by the time the defences of the stronghold were fully tested. In fact, without the citadel, the defenders would have been

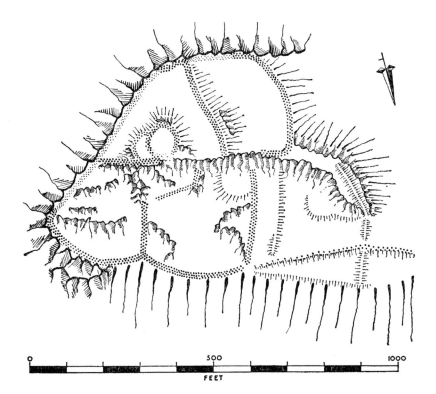

In this modern plan of Dundurn the dotted lines represent the locations of the later Pictish defences. A steep precipice on its southern and eastern sides meant that an attacker had to approach the fort from the west or north. Therefore the builders concentrated their defences to cover these approaches.

0   500   1000

FEET

unable to put up much of a fight. This alone suggests that the siege of Dundurn – an event worthy of mention in the *Annals of Ulster* – centred around the capture of the imposing citadel. In other words, the historical evidence suggests that the citadel was destroyed in the aftermath of the siege.

The third phase of Dundurn began in the aftermath of the destruction of the timber-laced citadel. The timber framing was destroyed by fire, the citadel demolished, and its stones strewn around the upper enclosure. Then the citadel was rebuilt, and the ramparts – if they had been demolished – were repaired. A massive rampart now ringed the upper terrace, which may or may not have been timber laced. Similar but less substantial ramparts were built around the three lower enclosures. This third phase can be loosely

D   NEXT PAGE: DUNDURN (DUN DURN), PICTISH 'NUCLEAR' FORTRESS, c. AD 683

Perhaps the most spectacular of all Early Historic strongholds in Scotland is Dundurn, located at the western end of Strathearn. According to the *Annals of Ulster* it was besieged in AD 683, by which stage the volcanic plug was crowned by a Pictish fortress. Like the Dal Riatan stronghold of Dunadd, the defences of Dun Durn were strengthened several times between the 6th and the 9th centuries AD. This reconstruction shows what the fortress might have looked like during the late 7th century AD, at the time it was besieged. While the *Annals* offer no clues as to who was doing the besieging, it is generally assumed that the Pictish fort was attacked by the Dal Riatan Scots – part of a wider conflict which saw their own fortress of Dunadd besieged in the same year.

The archaeological evidence is a little confusing, but it is assumed that the main entrance lay on the western side of the hill, where a steep track curved around the outer defences, then passed through a gate, and continued to wind its way in a spiral, up and around the hill, until it reached the small, round summit. A timber-laced stone-walled citadel stood there, but it is unclear whether this was covered by a roof. The courtyard below it, which formed the main enclosure of the fort, contained a well, and domestic buildings. Three lower enclosures might well have been purely defensive features – one covering the western approaches to the rock, and the other two descending towards the main entrance. During the excavations there, archaeologists found metalwork, leatherwork and glass – all signs that during this period Dundurn was an important site, either the stronghold of a Pictish sub-king or regional warlord, or possibly a high-status fortress protecting the western borders of the Pictish kingdom – a bastion against encroachment by the Dal Riatan Scots.

The inset shows just how imposing this fortress would have appeared to anyone approaching it from the south-west – the entire southern face of the hill consisted of a cliff-like crag.

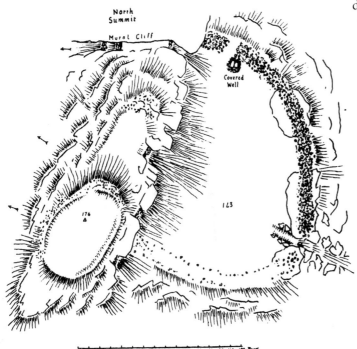

dated to the 8th century AD. The walls were subsequently repaired, and the fortress might well have remained in good repair until the mid 9th century AD or even AD 889, when – according to the *Scottish Regnal Lists* – King Girg, son of Dungal, died at Dundurn. Finds from this later period include a decorated leather shoe, fine-quality glass and metalwork, and metalworking tools. This all suggests that Dundurn remained a site of considerable importance until the very end of the Pictish period.

Dunadd

Like Dundurn, the Dal Riatan Scots' stronghold of Dunadd (or Dun Att) was also besieged in AD 683. While this seems unlikely to be a coincidence, the tantalizing joint entry in the *Annals of Ulster* fails to provide any further clues. What is clear is that by the late 7th century AD Dunadd was an important fortress – most likely the royal capital of the whole Dal Riatan kingdom.

Although Dunadd isn't the largest or even the most impressive 'nuclear' fort in Scotland, its historical associations, location and the multi-phase nature of the stronghold make it one of the most fascinating. The fort stands on a small rocky mound, like the boss of a shield. This mound was originally surrounded by marshland, which would have greatly enhanced its defensive value. One can only assume that it was originally designed to be accessible by boat. The defences surround the upper portion of the rocky boss, although broad, plateau-like areas on the lower levels may also have been fortified. Traces of a large rectangular building have been found on the plateau to the south of the summit, while traces of a slight wall surround the edge of the main defences, forming an even larger enclosure. This might well have marked the edge of the 'island'.

This is Christison's sketch of Dunadd, showing the features visible on the surface during his initial survey in 1904. Subsequent excavations revealed another inner courtyard, and the presence of ramparts around both the upper courtyard and the citadel.

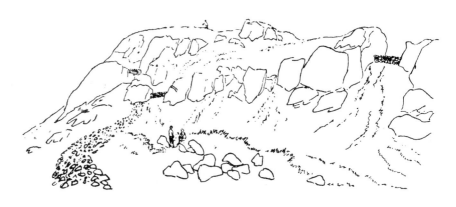

The eastern side of Dunadd, viewed from just inside the eastern enclosure. This sketch by Christison was drawn in 1904, when the fort was first properly investigated. The path leads to the rock-cut ascent to the upper courtyard, overlooked by the summit of the hill, where the stone-built citadel once stood.

The main area of the stronghold was clearly designed to take advantage of the craggy contours of the mound, and the leaf-shaped or tear-shaped summit is reached by a series of outer courtyards, built at various levels. The citadel on the summit (labelled Fort A by archaeologists) was surrounded by a substantial stone wall at least three metres (ten feet) thick, while similarly thick walls surround the outer courtyard area to the east (Fort B), the lower terrace (Fort D), and another outer terrace beyond that (Fort F). A possible extension to the upper courtyard – Fort C – lies below it, in the north-east corner of the site. This may have been nothing more than a wall, blocking the head of a ravine which climbs the hill at this point, and which separates the main fortified hill from a small northern peak or summit. Fort E is effectively the northern portion of Fort D (the lower terrace of Dunadd), and traces of walls that were once thought to divide them were most probably the remains of stone-built buildings. Fort E/F therefore comprises a habitable area – and the outer enclosure or courtyard of the fort.

This sketch plan by Christinson reveals how close the stronghold is to the river Add, although in the Early Historic period it is thought that the low-lying surrounding area was marsh, fed by the waters of the river. Dunadd was therefore an island.

The main entrance to the fort passes through this outer enclosure, and is cut out of the solid rock, forming an impressive and easily fortified passageway. Evidence of buildings can be found in this outer courtyard, together with a well. A narrow entrance leads to the inner courtyard, where a stone slab might have once formed part of a defended gateway. From these a narrow flight of stone steps cut into the rock curves up to a smaller upper courtyard, and the entrance to the citadel. Anyone climbing these steps would be exposed to missile fire from the defenders of the citadel, looming above them. Another narrow entrance leads from this upper courtyard into the citadel itself.

Unfortunately the site was extensively turned over by 19th-century and early 20th-century antiquarians, and as a result much of the archaeological information the site might have yielded has been lost. However, these keen amateurs uncovered broken moulds designed for the casting of ornaments, which indicated that Dunadd was an important site, possibly the seat of a Dal Riatan Scots' court. The importance of the site is also underlined by

The Dal Riatan royal stronghold of Dunadd (or Dun Att) rises from flat land which was once a marsh. The fortress expanded slightly over the centuries, but its core remained the stone-built citadel that stood on its highest point.

The outer eastern rampart of Dunadd 'nuclear' fort, viewed from outside the circuit, looking towards the smaller north summit of the hill. The area to the left, within the enclosure, was probably filled with domestic buildings and workshops.

the presence of several carvings in the upper courtyard. These include a 'footprint' and a carved rock basin, along with the carving of a Pictish-style boar, and a frustratingly indecipherable inscription written in Ogam script (a Celtic alphabet in runic form). It was assumed that, since the *Annals of Ulster* recorded that Dunadd was besieged in AD 683, the Picts might well have carved these after they captured the stronghold.

Like the Pictish stronghold of Dundurn, its Dal Riatan counterpart at Dunadd developed over the centuries, rather than emerging as a fully formed 'nuclear' fort in the 7th century AD. Archaeologists believe that some sort of fort existed at Dunadd during the Iron Age, as the earliest dateable evidence of fortifications predated the arrival of the Romans in Scotland. This may suggest that an earlier wall ringed the summit of the mound, but the evidence is questionable as later stonework may have intruded into a layer of Iron Age material. What we can say is that by the 4th or 5th centuries AD the summit was almost certainly ringed by a stone-built dun or citadel. This became Fort

E **DUNADD (DUN ATT), DAL RIATAN CAPITAL, c. AD 683**

One of the most important strongholds in Early Historic Scotland, Dunadd (or Dun Att in contemporary chronicles) was almost certainly the capital of the high kings of Dal Riata, a site which served both as a stronghold and as an administrative and cultural centre. Dunadd was a classic 'nuclear' fort, consisting of a central core, and a series of outer fortified enclosures or courtyards. Once again, while the archaeological evidence is fairly limited, the site has been thoroughly examined and it seems that the fort developed over time, as shown in the plate. Archaeologists are unsure whether the central citadel or even the upper courtyard were covered over with some form of roofing, so in this reconstruction two alternatives are offered – one with a

covered upper courtyard, and one with this forming an open area – a site for ceremonial activities.

Dunadd was besieged in AD 683, and while the *Annals of Ulster* don't provide any details, the presence of Pictish-style rock carvings within this inner courtyard area might suggest that the stronghold was besieged and captured by the Picts. At this time it is likely that a marsh surrounded the small hill of Dunadd, which meant that an attacker would first have to launch an assault by boat before storming the stronghold itself. The main plate shows the fort as it might have looked during a Pictish assault. The small inset shows the fort as it might have looked in the 6th century AD, before it developed into a strong, stone-built 'nuclear' fortress.

ABOVE The fortress of Dunadd is approached through a gully, cut into the rock, which forms a perfect 'killing ground' immediately in front of where the stronghold's gate would once have been. To either side stands the once-formidable eastern rampart.

BELOW The Dal Riatan royal capital of Dunadd developed over the centuries, from the citadel on its summit to the more complex 'nuclear' fort of the 7th and 8th centuries AD. Its builders also made good use of the natural defensive qualities of the rock on which the fortress was built.

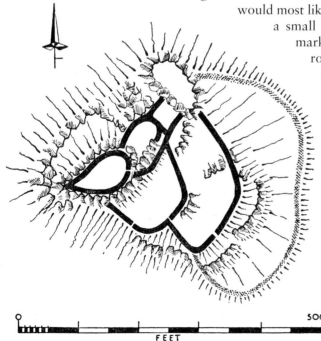

A of the 'nuclear' fort. The carved stone bowl and footprint may also date from this period.

The 'nuclear' fort developed when these earlier defences were extended to include the lower terraces of the mound. These areas might have been enclosed before, but this phase saw their encirclement by stone walls. The additional walls that can be accurately dated to this phase are those encircling the upper courtyard (Fort B), and the courtyard below it (Fort D). The dating of this phase is open to debate, but it seems likely that the 'nuclear' fort was in existence by the late 6th century AD, and therefore predated both the Pictish-style rock carving and inscription, and the siege of AD 683. It seems that the defences were expanded during the 8th or 9th centuries AD, and the walls may have been strengthened and rebuilt. This phase involved the demolition of the inner face of the Fort D rampart, and a new entrance was created spectacularly, passing through a natural rock gully. Despite the removal of the inner side of the Fort D enclosure, Dunadd was still a 'nuclear' fort, but one whose interior layout had been redesigned to suit the needs of a new generation of guardians. Evidence for the use of the site after the mid-9th century AD is a little fragmentary, but the general assumption is that, while it may well have remained occupied, Dunadd was no longer a site of great importance. In effect, political changes meant that the centre of power moved east and south, and this corner of what was now Alba became a region rather than an important kingdom in its own right.

If we return to the fort as it might have looked at the time of the siege of AD 683, it would have dominated the flat, marshy countryside around it, particularly if a visitor had to approach it by boat or causeway. After passing through the formidable entrance into the outer enclosure, the visitor would most likely have passed through what was effectively a small township – a place where workshops and marketplaces supplied the needs of the Dal Riatan royal household. After passing through a second gateway into the inner courtyard, the visitor would have climbed the stone-cut steps leading to the upper courtyard. This was certainly ringed by a substantial wall, as was the citadel that extended from it, but we are still unsure whether both of these structures were roofed over. If they were, then they would have formed large halls, worthy of a royal palace, where the warrior elite of Dal Riata could feast their way through the long winter.

This area also included the carved footprint and bowl, which might well have been areas of religious or secular importance – possibly the site where the Dal Riatan kings were inaugurated. This in itself suggests an open area, where a ceremony of this kind would be visible from the base of the hill. Finally a gate led into the teardrop-shaped citadel, which was most probably a roofed structure. Again, we know all too little about what went on here, but it is fairly safe to assume that this citadel summit formed the inner sanctum of the royal residence at Dunadd – the epicentre of the Dal Riatan kingdom. As archetypal 'nuclear' forts, it seems fairly obvious that both Dunadd and Dundurn made hierarchical use of space, and the higher up the hill you went, the more exalted were the occupants. However, even more so than Dundurn, which was a frontier fortress more than a royal stronghold, Dunadd was a capital – a place where power was enforced, and prestige maintained. It wasn't a capital in the modern sense – a town or city – but a fortified residence, where the infrastructure of kingship was concentrated.

THE PRINCIPLES OF DEFENCE

The Early Historic strongholds described here were hardly the most sophisticated of fortifications – they were nothing compared to the Roman legionary camps whose traces can still be found in southern and eastern Scotland, or even to the great Celtic hill forts that had their heyday before the coming of the Romans. However, for the most part they were compact, easily defended, and they made the best possible use of the natural defensive qualities of the terrain.

The defensive qualities of Celtic hill forts have already been described in an earlier Osprey book by the same author (Fortress 50: *The Forts of Celtic Britain*, Osprey Publishing Ltd: Oxford, 2006), and the military properties of some of those hill forts and promontory forts of this later period were virtually identical. For instance, the multivallate defences of Clatchard Craig or Burghead were similar to those earlier Celtic forts, where the outer network of banks and ditches served to slow and disorder an attack, rendering an assaulting force vulnerable to missile fire from the main rampart. At South Cadbury in southern England, a large pre-Roman hill fort was reused during the Early Historic period, and these older multivallate defences were little more than a hindrance. There, the main line of defence was the inner rampart, where a substantial wood and stone wall had been built, running around the inner perimeter of the site (see Fortress 80: *British Forts in the Age of Arthur*, Osprey Publishing Ltd: Oxford, 2008). This was almost certainly the form of defence that would have been found at Clatchard Craig or Traprain Law.

Obviously, promontory forts such as Burghead, Dunnottar or Portknockie exploited the natural defences offered by headlands, where only the narrow neck of the promontory needed to be fortified. They also offered sheltered havens for vessels, whether these were local fishing boats or larger raiding craft. The 18th-century plans of Burghead – before the building of the modern planned village – reveal a multivallate system with three substantial ramparts. The headland enclosed within these defences made Burghead the largest of all the Early Historic fortifications in Scotland, and one of the most formidable. Its timber-laced ramparts protected the innermost of these three lines of defence, which meant that the outer ditches and ramparts were little more than formidable obstacles, just like the outworks of a multivallate Celtic fort – the *murus gallicus* type of defences described by Julius Caesar in his *Commentaries on the Gallic War*. The difference was that at Burghead, these defences were built after the arrival of the Romans in Scotland.

The hill fort of Clatchard Craig overlooked the modern village of Newburgh in Fife. From the mid 1960s onwards quarrying destroyed the whole hill, but fortunately the site was surveyed and excavated before this industrial vandalism began. It was discovered that the earliest fortifications there dated from the Iron Age, but excavations revealed that the fort was reoccupied and refortified during the Early Historic period. During its final phase of development in the 8th century AD, the hill fort consisted of a series of six timber-laced stone-built ramparts, the innermost of which enclosed the main citadel of the fort, which backed onto a cliff.

These excavations suggested that while the fort resembled a typical Celtic hill fort, the Pictish stone defences had more in common with those found at Dundurn and Dunadd than other Scottish hill forts. They were substantial, and enclosed an area that suggested that the fort was of considerable importance. This status was reinforced by the inclusion of dressed stonework, taken from the nearby derelict Roman legionary fortress of Carpow. It has been suggested that this was a deliberate inclusion, designed to impart additional prestige on the fort by linking it to a half-forgotten era of order and stability.

The first inset shows a reconstruction of a Pictish roundhouse – evidence was found of several such structures within the inner perimeter of the fort. The second shows Clatchard Craig as it might have looked during an earlier phase of its development, in the mid-7th century AD.

Turin Hill near Forfar in Angus is often described as proto-Pictish – occupied before the historic emergence of the Picts in the 6th century AD. It consisted of this stone-built ring fort, set amid the hilltop defences of an earlier Iron Age fort.

At Burghead, the timber-laced stone wall was substantial – the remains of the western rampart of the inner citadel there suggest that these walls were 8.5m (28ft) thick. While these remains are three metres (ten feet) high, we can assume that at the time of their use they were considerably more formidable. These dimensions are similar to those at Dundurn. There the timber-laced rampart of the upper fort was approximately eight metres (26ft) wide, while the similarly timber-laced stone defences of the citadel on the summit of the hill were four metres (13ft) thick. Today, the slopes of Dundurn appear to be covered in scree and boulders. In fact, these have been proven to be the remains of the ramparts, which were either deliberately knocked down or collapsed over the centuries. This suggests that the defences were once very

Clatchard Craig, Pictish hill fort, c. AD 700

Moncreiffe Hill (Monid Craebe) overlooking the modern city of Perth was the site of an important Pictish hill fort. It may have been a regional capital, possibly the seat of the Pictish sub-kingdom of Fortiu. The later Pictish palace at Forteviot lies only a few kilometres to the west, which reinforces the importance of this area to the Picts.

substantial indeed. In both cases, we might safely assume that the walls reached a height of at least four metres (13ft), which, when augmented by ditches and outer banks at Burghead, or a steep slope at Dundurn, would have made them extremely difficult obstacles to take through assault.

In 'nuclear' forts the positioning of the walls was important. Outworks were often sited to cover the only easy route to the main gate of the fort, so that defenders could assail the attackers with missiles as they approached it. For instance, although the exact location and appearance of the gate leading into the Dundurn defences is unclear, the obvious approach was by means of a track that curved up the western side of the hill, overlooked by the defenders on the crags above and in each successive courtyard of the fort itself. It has also been suggested that small bulwarks on the north-western, western and south-western sides provided platforms for missile troops, in the event of a determined attack. They therefore resembled the ravelins and detached bastions of 18th-century fortifications, and were designed to delay rather than to stop an attacker. Similarly, at Dunadd each courtyard is overlooked by others, and the steps leading to the upper courtyard are sited almost directly beneath the southern wall of the main citadel. All this made an assault a frustrating and a daunting prospect.

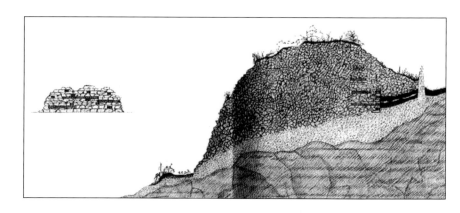

A cross-section of the remains of the ramparts of Burghead, recorded before they were demolished in the early 19th century. These show traces of timber cross-bracing.

Finally, the weakest point of any fort of this kind was the gateway. This is why in these Early Historic forts the approach to the gateway was either covered by flanking defences, or else the approach leading to the gateway was restricted, as was the case at Dunadd, where the later fort was entered through a gate at the end of a narrow, rock-cut gully. It was also sited carefully to make the best possible use of the terrain to slow down or constrict an attacking force. The number of entrances was also restricted, usually to just one main gate, such as was almost certainly the case at Cairn Phadrig, where St Columba found the gate barred on his arrival there.

While there is almost no archaeological evidence to tell us what these gateways looked like, enough information from similar sites in Southern England and on the continent of Europe suggest that they would have been relatively simple wooden affairs, with a double-leaved gate secured by crossbars when it was closed. Given the scale of the walls at Dunadd, Burghead and other Early Historic sites, these would have been fairly large and substantial, and may have been covered by a walkway, or some form of wooden entrance tower. This, of course, would have made them even more formidable entranceways. Anyone trying to climb the hill at Dundurn today will appreciate just how well all this came together – well-sited walls and entranceways, restricted or steep approaches, and fortifications that made the best possible use of the natural defensive qualities of the terrain.

THE LIVING SITES

Strongholds in the political landscape

The strongholds described here were much more than mere fortifications. Many were also political and administrative centres – the power bases of kings, sub-kings or regional warlords. A few might also have combined these secular functions with an importance as a religious site. For instance, it has been suggested that the strange rock carvings on the plateau of Dunadd were used as a place of inauguration of the Dal Riatan Scots high kings, and also as a place of regular religious observance. While many of these associations are ambiguous, at least the historical records tell us something about the way these important sites functioned within the political framework of Early Historic Scotland.

We know from the emphasis placed upon it in the historical records that Dunadd was the major centre of secular power within the Dal Riatan kingdom, as well as being an important military stronghold. Similarly, Adomnan, bishop of Iona from AD 679 to 704, in his *Life of Columba* recorded that the early Christian saint journeyed up Loch Ness into the kingdom of the northern Picts, where he met King Bridei, a Pictish ruler. This encounter took place at *munitio Brudei* (Bridei's fortress), which means that wherever it was, this fortress was also a royal stronghold. While both the site of Urquhart Castle on Loch Ness and Craig Phadrig beside Inverness have been proposed, the likelihood is that the encounter took place at the latter site. This would mean that Craig Phadrig was not only an important *munitio*, but also most probably the political centre of the northern half of the Pictish kingdoms. Adomnan, writing more than a century after this late 6th century encounter, had probably never seen the stronghold he described, and any chronicler who has his saintly hero encounter the Loch Ness monster on his journey should be viewed with a fair degree of suspicion. However, Adomnan is quite specific that the *munitio* had a two-sided wooden gate, which was

barred on Columba's approach. He is also clear that the fort also contained the hall of the king.

One of our problems is that we don't know how these Early Historic kingdoms and sub-kingdoms were organised. Yes, we know that Pictland included northern and eastern Scotland, and extended as far south as the Firth of Forth. We can place its border with the territory of the Scots somewhere in Druim Alban, the mountainous spine that runs through the Scottish Highlands. Unfortunately, we know little about how this Pictish territory was ruled. The Grampian Mountains formed a natural barrier between northern and southern Pictland, and near Dunnottar the southern edge of this high ground – known as 'The Mounth' comes within a few miles of the sea. Just glancing at the map will show that Dunnottar was a strategic location, sited on the border of these two regions – the lands of the northern and southern Picts. Bede wrote about the lands of the northern and southern Picts – and pointed out that the southerners were converted to Christianity long before Columba attempted to convert Bridei's northern kingdom. Beyond that we lack hard evidence.

Historians have claimed that the Pictish kingdoms were composed of seven provinces, but this is inferred from the historical evidence rather than stated. The king of the Northern Picts – a man like Bridei – may well have been independent from his southern counterpart, but we simply don't know. He almost certainly ruled over sub-kings – for instance, those of Orkney, which, as far as we can tell, formed its own political sub-division.

The *rex Fortren* (king of Fortriu) is mentioned in contemporary annals, which seem to indicate that this area was the heartland of the Picts – a territory which until recently has been associated with Southern Pictland. Recently scholars have suggested that it lay further north – and lay along the coast of the Moray Firth. In other words it was the area ruled by Bridei. This association is strengthened by records in the *Annals of Ulster*, which record that the Norsemen ravaged the coast of Fortriu. This meant that the fortresses of Craig Phadrig, Burghead and Dunnottar lay in the lands of Fortriu, while those of Dundurn, Moncreiffe and Clatchard Craig formed part of the southern kingdom – probably in the provinces recorded as Circinn (possibly now Perth and Angus) and Fib (now Fife).

We reach firmer ground further to the west, where the Scots of Dal Riata may have had their origins recorded in Irish myth, but their subsequent political organization was better recorded than that of their Pictish neighbours. It stretched as far as Druim Alban in the east, the Firth of Clyde to the south, and extended northwards into the mountains of what is now Lochaber. Dal Riata almost certainly had its political centre at Dunadd, but it was also divided into sub-kingdoms: Cenél nOengusa in Islay and the surrounding islands (augmented by Cenél Comgaill in the 8th century AD), Cenél nGabráin in Kintyre and Cenél Loairn in Argyll. Dunadd lay between these two mainland regions, but it was almost certainly controlled by the rulers of Cenél Loairn. Similarly the fortress of Dunollie (outside the modern town of Oban) probably formed the main *munitio* of Cenél nGabráin.

To the south, Alt Clut (Dumbarton) was the political centre of the Britons of Strathclyde, and remained so until its capture by the Norsemen in the late 9th century AD. To the east lay the old lands of the Goddodin, who – if the medieval Welsh poem *y Goddodin* is to be believed – died almost to a man, in battle against the Angles outside Catraeth (Catterick) around AD 600. Their territory would have included the fortress of Dun Eidin (where Edinburgh Castle now stands), and almost certainly the powerful Early Historic hill fort of Dalmahoy a few kilometres to the west. Further to the east lay the even older hill fort of Traprain Law, which remained a regional stronghold until its territory fell to the Angles in the mid-7th century AD. As for the Angles themselves, their only known stronghold north of Bamburgh was Doon Hill near Dunbar, which was more of a palace than a stronghold.

What is clear is that many of the major Early Historic fortresses mentioned here served two purposes – as military stronghold and political centre. While the role of some of these such as Dunadd, Alt Clut and Craig Phadrig is reasonably clear, others are less so. Dundurn for example was clearly an important stronghold, with dwelling houses on its summit, and

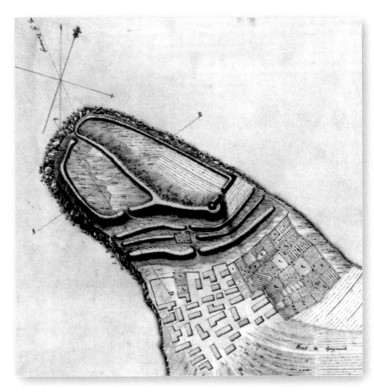

General Roy's map of Burghead, drawn in 1793, showed the basic outlines of the fort, complete with its multivallate outer defences. Much of these outer defences were demolished a few years later, and today only the inner walls of the fort still remain.

dominating the western approaches to the lush and fertile valley of Strathearn. It also blocked an important passage through Druim Alban, leading to the heart of southern Pictland behind it. The discovery of high-value finds at Dalmahoy suggests that this Midlothian stronghold was also an important political centre, but we know little about the role the fort itself played in the political development of the region, let alone its role as an administrative centre. Like so much of Early Historic evidence, it suggests what might have been, without actually giving us any hard information.

Strongholds as royal bastions

During this period all of the four peoples who inhabited Early Historic Scotland – the native Britons and Picts, and the incoming Scots and Angles – all conformed to the same pattern of social hierarchy associated with warrior societies. All four were divided into kindreds or sub-kingdoms, and most were involved in civil wars as well as larger struggles against their neighbours. The warrior caste is glorified in contemporary heroic poetry, which is at odds with the more serious record provided by contemporary annals, which list major battles, sieges and the destruction of strongholds.

You only need to look at the romance surrounding the medieval knight, and then to compare this to the histories of chroniclers such as Froissart to realize that the warrior caste might see itself in a heroic light, but this only formed part of the bigger picture of warfare during the period. Battles such as Nechtansmere (AD 685) or sieges such as the fall of Alt Clut (AD 870) had major political implications and were far removed from the romance of heroic poetry. Yes, the kingdoms were ruled by a warrior elite, whose social and military structure was clearly defined. Territories were ruled by means of a pyramid of high kings, sub-kings, regional rulers, warriors and common people. All could be called upon for military service, but the commoners were there to make up numbers, not to have their deeds recorded in epic poetry.

This suggests a society where the king, sub-kings or rulers held court, surrounded by warrior retinues. All of these were funded through levies of produce or through taxation, and the burden was borne by the lower strata of society – the farmers, fishermen and tradesmen. With a few exceptions such as Tarbert, Doon Hill or Forteviot, these courts were located in strongholds where the warrior elite could dominate the surrounding countryside, produce or taxes could be gathered and stored, and winter preparations could be made for a new season of campaigning.

It is clear that status was important. These strongholds often looked imposing, and this had social as well as military benefits for their owners. After all, most farmers in Early Historic Scotland wanted to till their soil in peace, and these kings, warriors and strongholds provided stability. Some might even have enhanced their authority by drawing on dim memories of a lost golden age – this may explain the use of Roman stones in the walls of the Pictish hill fort of Clatchard Craig, taken from the nearby ruins of the abandoned Roman legionary fortress of Carpow. Other links were even more explicit – for instance, Pictish fortifications have been associated with the Roman legionary fortress of Bertha on the river Almond, on the northern outskirts of Perth, and on the fringe of the 1st century AD legionary fortress of Inchtuthil, several kilometres to the north.

The medieval pattern was that a king would tour his kingdom, visiting castles and collecting tribute as he went. This was almost certainly practised in these Early Historic kingdoms, where the collection of provisions, weaponry and taxes would have helped sustain both the dignity of the high king or sub-king, and feed and clothe his retinue. This suggests that some fortresses would have been permanently occupied by a royal official (a *praefectus* in Latin) and his warband, who would rule through his own retinue, on behalf of his king. A royal visit would involve the renewal of his fealty, and the consumption of the goods he had collected.

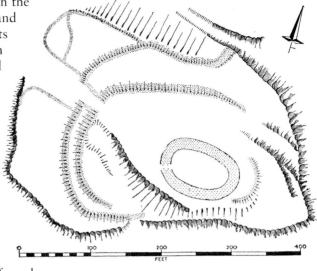

Archaeological evidence from sites as diverse as Burghead, Dunadd, Alt Clut (Dumbarton), Dunnottar, Dundurn and Urquhart all suggest that livestock was gathered within the outer walls of these strongholds, and many show evidence of both domestic life and the existence of workshops, producing weapons, jewellery and ceramics. Pottery finds indicate that many of these strongholds benefited from trade, as many of the ceramics had their origins far outside the stronghold's hinterland. Clearly these forts played a major part in contemporary society, and were much more than mere military strongholds.

For instance, during the excavation of the Pictish fort of Dundurn in Strathearn, the enclosure immediately below the small upper citadel (where presumably a great stone-walled hall once stood), the archaeologists discovered the remains of wattle and daub buildings, with what might have been workshops and animal enclosures intermingled with domestic structures. The obvious impression is that of a court, where these buildings housed the warriors and their families or servants, as well as the merchants, traders and manufacturers who enjoyed their patronage. Similarly, Burghead contained two enclosures, and one was almost certainly a similar area, where the hall of a ruler was surrounded by outer buildings containing his retinue, and those who made their living from supplying his court with its needs.

Dumyat hill fort near Stirling was a proto-Pictish fort, which may well have been a regional centre of power before the development of the Pictish kingdoms. A post-Roman ring fort sits on the summit of the 418m-high (1,370ft) hill, amid the earlier Iron Age ramparts.

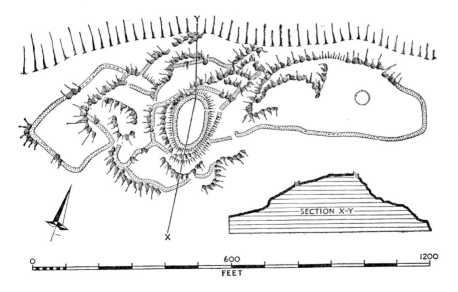

The hill fort of Dalmahoy near Livingston in Midlothian was one of the first sites identified as a 'nuclear' fort – a definition whose use was then applied to similar strongholds at Dunadd and Dundurn. Unfortunately we know very little about this complex site, save that it was in use during the Early Historic period.

Another aspect is the religious nature of some of these centres. Burghead and Dunadd have both been associated with finds of a possible religious nature, while others – most notably the strongholds of Montcrieffe, Clatchard Craig and Dundurn – all have identifiable Christian sites close by, suggesting a close link between these strongholds and seats of both secular and religious power that existed both before and after the coming of Christianity to Scotland.

While a lot remains unclear, we can at least glimpse something of the importance of these strongholds in contemporary life. They were fortresses, administrative centres, and sometimes they functioned as religious sites as well. Many benefited from trade, industry and the demands of a warrior aristocracy. While we don't understands exactly what life was like within their walls, at least we know enough to see just how important these strongholds were.

THE SITES IN WAR

What we know about the military role played by the strongholds comes from a few scant mentions in the written records. The *Annals of Ulster* and a handful of other Scottish and Irish historical sources provide little more than dates, telling us when certain forts were besieged or destroyed. What this doesn't usually tell us is the far more illuminating information of who was doing the besieging, and why. Still, the importance given to these dates and attacks shows us that the sieges of these strongholds were important events, worthy of particular mention.

Given that many of these strongholds were also the power centres of high kings, sub-kings or local warlords, this importance was political as well as

RIGHT
A general view of Dumbarton Rock, pictured during the 1970s, before the docks to the north became reclaimed and the site reused. During the Early Historic period the rock was known as Alt Clut (the Rock of the Clyde), and it served as the principal stronghold of the Britons of Strathclyde.

OPPOSITE
The political landscape of Early Historic Scotland, *c.* AD 800

Political boundaries in Scotland, *c.* AD 800

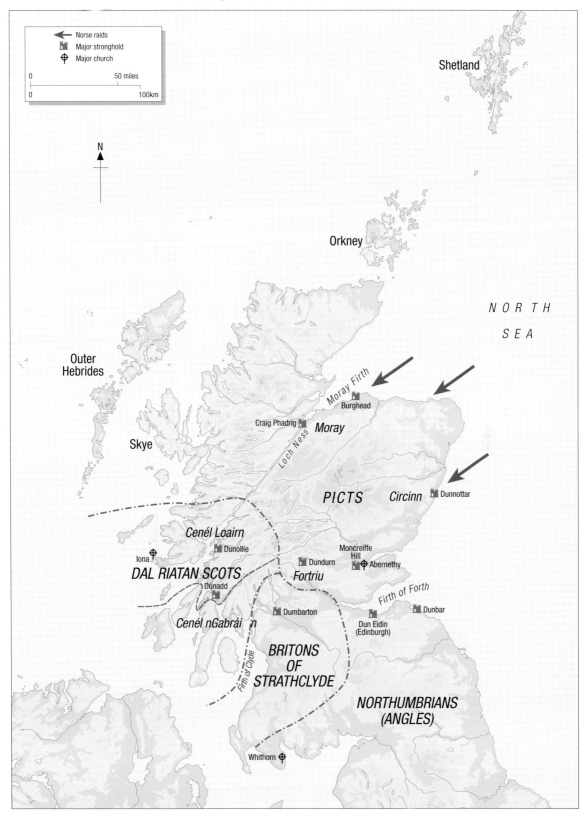

Norse raids

Major stronghold

Major church

0   50 miles

0   100km

N

Shetland

Orkney

NORTH

SEA

Outer
Hebrides

Skye

Moray Firth

Burghead

Craig Phadrig

Moray

Loch Ness

PICTS

Circinn

Dunnottar

Cenél Loairn

Dunollie

Iona

DAL RIATAN SCOTS

Dunadd

Moncreiffe
Hill

Dundurn

Abernethy

Fortriu

Firth of Forth

Cenél nGabráin

Dumbarton

Dunbar

Dun Eidin
(Edinburgh)

BRITONS
OF
STRATHCLYDE

Firth of Clyde

NORTHUMBRIANS
(ANGLES)

Whithorn

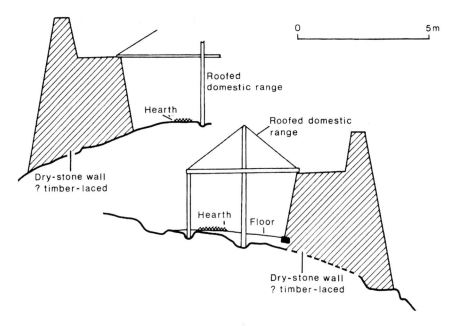

The promontory fort at Urquhart on the shores of Loch Ness was excavated during the 1980s. This reconstruction produced as a result of this work suggests the possible appearance of timber buildings built behind the walls of the small fortress.

military – these fortifications served as administrative centres, storehouses, and rallying points for the defending kingdom. This also explains why the few open battles mentioned in the historical records were often associated with fortifications. For example, the battle of Nechtansmere (AD 685), fought between the Picts and the invading Northumbrians took place near 'Dun Nechtan', or Nechtan's fort – presumably the stronghold of a local Pictish warlord on Dunnichen Hill in Angus. Similarly, during a Pictish civil war in AD 728, the battle fought at Monid Craebe almost certainly took place in front of Moncreiffe Hill, an important royal centre and stronghold overlooking the river Earn, just south of the modern city of Perth. In other words, fortifications served as the focal point for warfare during the Early Historic period.

Sieges played a prominent part in warfare. The historic records provide a string of these, from the siege of the unidentified *Rithe* (from the word 'rath', or enclosure) in AD 641 (and again in AD 703), to the capture, sacking and destruction of Alt Clut (Dumbarton) at the hands of the Norsemen in AD 870. While most of these strongholds can be identified, a few cannot. Those that can include the Pictish fortifications of Dunnottar (besieged in AD 681 and 694), Dundurn (AD 683) and Dun Baittie (Dunbeath, in AD 680), the Dal Riatan Scots' strongholds of Dunadd (AD 683 and 736), Dunollie (AD 698 and 701) and Dunaverty (AD 712), and the Dal Riatan palace of Tarbert (AD 712 and 730). The Goddodin fortress of Dun Eidin (Edinburgh) was captured by the Angles in AD 638, and presumably Dalmahoy and Traprain Law fell around the same time. The last British stronghold of Alt Clut (Dumbarton) was besieged in AD 756, and then captured, sacked and destroyed in AD 870.

This list of sieges only tells part of the story. During the campaigns of the Dal Riatan high king Aedan mac Gabráin in the late 6th century AD, Alt Clut (Dumbarton) was besieged by his Dal Riatan Scots army. The stronghold of King Riderch 'the Generous' (Rhydderch Hael) of the Strathclyde Britons was besieged until the defenders 'were left without food nor drink nor beast alive'. This siege was deemed so remarkable for its length and ferocity that it featured in the Welsh triad *Tier Drut Heirua Ynys Brydein* ('Three unrestrained ravages of the island of Britain'). The suggestion here is that the defenders were starved into submission, and that this was an unusual end to a siege. This implies that the defenders usually yielded before this, or the attackers gave up and went home.

A similar outcome occurred during another siege of Alt Clut in AD 756, when the Strathclyde fortress was invested by an unlikely coalition of Picts and Northumbrians. According to Symeon of Durham, in his *Historia Regum Anglorum*: 'King Eadbertht [of Northumbria] and Unuist, King of the Picts led an army to the city of the Alcwith [Alt Clut], and hence the Britons accepted terms there, on the first day of the month of August.' While this outcome was relatively bloodless, the siege, capture and sacking of the British fortress in AD 870 was a far more destructive affair. This time the siege lasted for four months, so clearly the defenders had time to lay in provisions before the Norsemen invested Alt Clut. This time though, there would be no meek capitulation. The Vikings captured the fortress, and 'took all the goods that were inside … a great host was taken out into captivity'. The prisoners included King Artgal of Strathclyde, who died in captivity in Dublin two year later. The Vikings reputedly needed 200 longships to carry the slaves and the plunder back to their base in Dublin, and destroyed the fortress when they left.

This was a siege – *obsessio* in the Latin script of the records. However, it was far removed from the methodical, patient siegecraft of Vauban or the other 18th-century masters. The options available to an attacking force were limited. The defenders could be starved out, but only if the attackers were able to live off the land, and the defenders had been unable to stockpile supplies. The stronghold could be assaulted, but while the records refer to sieges, there are no accounts of fortresses being taken by storm. While this may well have happened – after all, it fits in with the heroic nature of warfare during the period – a combination of the lack of suitable siege equipment, and the well-sited nature of many of these forts would have conspired to make such attacks unlikely to succeed.

It was also clear that some form of unwritten code existed, governing the way sieges were conducted. If medieval examples apply, this would involve summoning the defenders to surrender, personal challenges, and rules governing the treatment of prisoners and the plundering of goods. This suggests why exceptions such as the three sieges of Dumbarton mentioned earlier were considered so out of the ordinary that their outcome was noted in such detail. The Norsemen of course would have ignored any such conventions, either when attacking Dumbarton or during their assaults on the coastal defences of the Pictish kingdom.

An option open to the attacker was the destruction of a fort through burning. Archaeologists have long held that the existence of so many vitrified forts in Scotland suggests that this wasn't a technique to strengthen the defences, but the result of deliberate slighting of the defences after their capture, or during a siege. As we have seen, the majority of Early Historic defences in Scotland were built the same way, with stone (and in some cases rubble) being used to fill a timber framework. Outer skins of well-laid stone gave the impression of a well-constructed wall, but these defences had one great flaw. The timbers used to construct them were usually exposed, and could therefore be set on fire. Although experiments have shown that this was difficult to achieve, once a fire started the results

Burghead, Pictish royal centre and stronghold, c. AD 750

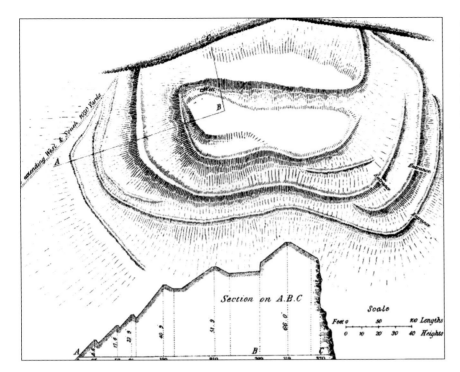

Although the Pictish hill fort of Clatchard Craig has been destroyed by quarrying, this plan indicates just how extensive a site it was. The fort itself backed onto a cliff which ran along its northern edge, and the stone-built defences radiated out from a central core.

would be spectacular. The defences would crumble, as the vitrified rubble would collapse into the spaces left by the destroyed timber. The effect would have been the same as if artillery had been used to batter a breach in the defences – a path would have been created for the attackers to assault the fortress.

The defences of Burghead were burned in this manner, suggesting a dramatic conclusion to a Norse attack. Similar destruction at Dundurn has been dated to the time of the siege of the stronghold in AD 683, suggesting that this was either the cause of the fort's capture, or the result of its deliberate destruction by the attacking force. Other forts suffered the same fate – the Dal Riatan stronghold of Dunolie (AD 685 and again in AD 698), the unidentified fort of *Creich* when it was attacked by the Picts in AD 736, and of course the deliberate destruction of Alt Clut after its capture by the Norsemen in AD 870. Of course, what archaeology can't always tell us is whether these vitrified remains were accidental or deliberate, or whether it took place during a siege or in its immediate aftermath. That said, we can surmise that this

G BURGHEAD, PICTISH ROYAL CENTRE AND STRONGHOLD, C. AD 750

The most impressive of all Pictish fortifications, the large promontory fort at Burghead was a multivallate fort, with the fortifications spanning the neck of the small headland, enclosing an area of approximately 28,000 square metres (2.8 hectares, or seven acres). This area was divided by an earthen bank into two sections – one higher and slightly smaller than the other. Both of these compounds had its own separate entrance in the outer wall, with no evidence of an internal gateway between them inside the fortress itself. This suggests some form of hierarchical use, the higher enclosure service some important secular or spiritual function.

Unfortunately, most of these defences were demolished in the late 18th century to make way for a planned village.

Fortunately, a combination of archaeological investigation and a detailed late 18th-century plan allow us to reconstruct these multivallate defences with some accuracy.

The inset shows a reconstructed cross-section of the main rampart at Burghead, showing how the defences used timber to provide a basic framework, fastened together using iron nails. A stone rubble was used as a filler, and the wall was faced with solid dry-stone walling. The scene depicts the defences under assault by a Norse raiding party during the mid 8th century BC. The bull carving is one of several found at Burghead, and the symbol may have had a special secular or religious meaning for the Pictish inhabitants.

damage was the result of warfare – the sheer number of vitrified remains of this kind make any other conclusion unlikely.

Forts appear prominently in the historic records, but never more so than during the early 8th century AD. The campaigns of Unuist, son of Uurguist, king of the Picts seem to have centred on the siege or the defence of strongholds, some of which remain unidentified. For instance, Dungal, high king of Dal Riata, was wounded during the siege and subsequent destruction of the Scots' fort of *Dun Leithfinn*, the site of which has never been satisfactorily indentified. In AD 736 Unuist's brother Talorgan defeated a Dal Riatan army a few miles from Dunadd, allowing Unuist to storm and capture the Scots' citadel. In modern military operations, this would have been a decisive blow. However, the Dal Riatan Scots were allowed to survive, and within a decade the tide had turned, and it was the Picts rather than the Scots who were on the defensive. This either suggests a half-hearted approach to warfare during the period – heroic in nature rather than decisive – or that Unuist was simply intervening in an already existing power struggle within Dal Riata. In either case, it shows that the Picts lacked the capacity to deliver a knockout blow, or to rule conquered territory through the occupation of captured strongholds.

The Norse of course, didn't play by the rules. Their attacks on the Pictish coast during the 8th and 9th centuries AD correspond with the waning of Pictish power and the devastation of the Pictish heartland. Coastal fortifications were only part of the answer. They were vulnerable, and while Portknockie might have been built and Burghead refurbished to help defend the Pictish kingdom, there is no evidence that either proved much of a deterrent. The archaeological evidence suggests that both were captured and destroyed. Similarly, in AD 900 King Donmal, son of Constantine, was captured and killed after a Norse siege of Dunnottar. Raids into the hinterland would have undermined the ability of the Picts to feed, arm and house their warrior elite, and this in turn would have reduced the ability of the Pictish kings to react to these raids. In the end, their fortifications did little to protect the Picts from invasion and annexation. Their burnt remains stand as testimony to both the ferocity of the Norsemen, and the vagaries of Early Historic power.

AFTERMATH

When the end came, the Pictish kingdom disappeared so swiftly and with so little fuss that historians and archaeologists have puzzled over its demise ever since. In AD 800 Early Historic Scotland was divided between four peoples – the Picts, the Dal Riatan Scots, the Britons and the Angles (or Northumbrians). The Northumbrians were divided and in decline, while the Britons of Strathclyde were hard-pressed to hold on to the territory they owned.

The Norse raids began in the AD 790s, and one of their by-products was the destruction of many of the written records held in monasteries such as Iona and Lindisfarne. This left gaps in the historical record, which makes the collapse of the Pictish kingdom all the harder to understand. Certainly the Norse raids weakened the Pictish kingdom and created political instability. It seems that political opportunists made the most of this, the most notable of which was Cinaed mac Ailpín (often anglicized to Kenneth MacAlpin, r. AD 810–58), who in AD 843 managed to secure control of the Pictish kingship. He was already a minor ruler of Dal Riata, and by his death mac Ailpín effectively ruled a joint kingdom – a union that eventually emerged as Alba – the kingdom of Scotland.

During this century of strife the great fortresses fell one by one, and were destroyed. The destruction of Alt Clut (Dumbarton) in AD 870 marked the beginning of the end for the Britons of Strathclyde. Within a few decades the kingdom was little more than a client state of Alba. In AD 884, Earl Sigurd of Orkney captured Burghead, and 16 years later the Pictish king, Domnall son of Constantine, died when Dunnottar fell to King Harald 'Fairhair' of Norway.

The promontory fort at Portknockie was protected on three sides by the sea, and on its landward side by a natural gully. This modern track might well follow the line of the original approach to the fort, leading to a gate in its landward side.

By then the political landscape had changed. The transformation of Dal Riata and the Pictish kingdom into Alba – Scotland – was well underway, and the coronation of King Constantine II at Scone in AD 906 marked the effective culmination of this process. By then the nature of the Norse raids had changed, and the Vikings began to consolidate their control of Orkney and the north of Scotland, or continued their raids further south, into England, Wales and Ireland. The new enemy of Alba was the Anglo-Saxon kingdom to the south, and while Constantine II would wage war against the Northumbrians, his old Pictish and Dal Riatan strongholds were abandoned.

Due to their strategic location some of these Early Historic fortifications – particularly those in the lowlands of Scotland – would be strengthened and rebuilt. Dunnottar, Stirling and Edinburgh would become medieval castles, as the natural defensive qualities of these sites stood the test of time. Other once-powerful strongholds, such as Dunadd, Dalmahoy and Dundurn, were abandoned until the ravages of antiquarians and archaeologists would disturb their pastoral tranquillity.

THE SITES TODAY

With hundreds of sites, many of them small, and on private land, this selection of Early Historic fortifications in Scotland isn't a complete list. One of the most comprehensive gazetteers of sites can be found on-line, in the appendix to an article published in the *Proceedings of the Society of Antiquaries in Scotland* (1990), entitled 'Excavations at Alt Clut, Clyde Rock, Strathclyde, 1974–75'. Incidentally, this is one of a series of five detailed

The stones used in this inner rampart at Clatchard Craig show just how rough these timber-laced, stone-built dry-stone walls would have been. However, dressed stone was also brought to the site from the ruins of the derelict Roman fortress of Carpow.

The inner defences at Clatchard Craig, photographed during their excavation in 1960. The slope beyond the trenches represented the site of a defensive rampart, which overlooked another lower enclosure.

excavation reports written by Professor Alcock that can be found online. The other sites covered are Dundurn, Dunollie, St Abb's Head, Urquhart and Dunnottar.

Rather than a full gazetteer then, this list represents a selection of key sites, concentrating on ones which are accessible to the public, or which play an important part in the story. In most cases any tour will be self-guided – an exploratory ramble through the crumbling and overgrown remains. A handful of sites are owned and maintained by national bodies, such as Historic Scotland. In these cases, the sites are well described, with information points and guidebooks. Unfortunately, in most of these cases, the real attraction is a medieval castle built on top of the Early Historic fortifications. That means that – as in many of these sites – there is little to see of the old Early Historic fortifications. Still, the main benefit of any visit to one of these sites is to be able to stand on the same hilltop or promontory, and to imagine what it might have looked like in the days of the Picts, the Dal Riatan Scots or the Britons.

Forts

Brough of Birsay, Orkney

This small tidal island lying off the West Mainland of Orkney was occupied by the Picts, and may well have been a major centre of Pictish power in the islands. A nearby Pictish settlement at Butquoy on the mainland was in existence at the same time, and helps reinforce the theory that Birsay was an important secular or religious centre during the Early Historic period. The Brough of Birsay became a Norse settlement and religious centre during the 10th century. The site is maintained by Historic Scotland, and is open to the public – tides permitting.
www.historic-scotland.gov.uk
www.undiscoveredscotland.co.uk/westmainland/broughofbirsay/index.html

Burghead, Morayshire

Although the large Pictish promontory fort was partly destroyed in the early 19th century, when the planned village was built over the outer defences, enough remains of the stronghold to give visitors an impression of how it might have looked. A new visitor centre provides an excellent overview of Burghead during the Early Historic period, and interpretation panels in what was once the interior of the fort provide additional information. The site is open all the year round, but the visitor centre is only open from May until September.
www.burghead.com

Craig Phadrig, Invernesshire

This impressive Early Historic hill fort lies on the outskirts of Inverness, on land owned by the Forestry Commission. It may well have been the stronghold of the Pictish king Bridei, who was converted to Christianity by St Columba in the 6th century AD. Public access is by way of a woodland path, and interpretive panels are provided. Although the hilltop is surrounded by trees, enough remains of the site for visitors to gain an impression of what this important early Pictish stronghold might have looked like.
http://her.highland.gov.uk/SingleResult.aspx?uid='MHG3809'

Dalmahoy Hill, Midlothian

This impressive 'nuclear' fort covers the elongated summit of the hill, which dominates the surrounding area, particularly on its southern side. Kaimes Hill beside it was occupied during the Iron Age, but had fallen into disuse by the time the Early Historic stronghold on Dalmahoy Hill was built. The site has been excavated, but, despite its impressive location, few visible traces can be seen of the defences. The site is accessible on foot, and the views are well worth the steep climb to the summit – once the site of a stone-built citadel.
www.cyberscotia.com/ancient-lothian/leaves/places/dalmahoy-hillfort.html
www.megalithic.co.uk/article.php?sid=22888

Doon Hill, East Lothian

This small Early Historic fortified hall lies three kilometres (two miles) south of Dunbar, a rare example of a Northumbrian settlement in Scotland. The site is contained in a field, maintained by Historic Scotland, who provide year-round access. Historic Scotland call the site 'Doonehill historic homestead'. Interpretation is provided by means of information panels.
www.historic-scotland.gov.uk
www.undiscoveredscotland.co.uk/dunbar/doonhill/index.html

Dumbarton Rock, Dunbartonshire

This spectacular rocky crag looms over the river Clyde, just below the modern town of Dumbarton, a few miles up river from Glasgow. Unfortunately, there is no visible trace of the Early Historic defences, which were comprehensively destroyed by the Norsemen in AD 870. The site was refortified in the medieval period, and today the rock is dominated by 18th-century fortifications. To help interpret the way the site might have looked when it was an Early Historic stronghold, visitors might want to download the late Professor Alcock's excavation report before exploring the site. Dumbarton Castle is owned and maintained by Historic Scotland, and opening details and visitor information can be found on their website.
www.historic-scotland.gov.uk
www.undiscoveredscotland.co.uk/dumbarton/dumbartoncastle/index.html
http://canmore.rcahms.gov.uk/en/site/43376/details/dumbarton+castle/
Excavation report: http://ads.ahds.ac.uk/catalogue/adsdata/PSAS_2002/pdf/vol_120/120_095_149.pdf

Dunadd, Argyllshire

Probably the royal capital of the Dal Riatan Scots, Dunadd is sited on a small rocky hill that rises from a flat plain, making it an unusual but impressive location for an Early Historic stronghold. The ruins are both visible and imposing, and the site is well maintained by Historic Scotland, who provide free access and information by means of informative panels. This is one of the few unspoilt Early Historic sites in Scotland, and is well worth the detour to this tucked-away corner of western Scotland. Of course, in its heyday, Dunadd was the very epicentre of Scottish power.
www.historic-scotland.gov.uk
www.undiscoveredscotland.co.uk/kilmartin/dunadd/index.html

Dundurn, Perthshire

Unlike Dunadd, this important Pictish stronghold isn't officially open to the public, although the hill remains a popular attraction for ramblers. The

120m-high (394ft) rocky crag is also known as St Fillans Hill. In theory, permission should be sought from the landowner, and the hill is best climbed from its western face, accessible from a track beyond the local golf course. In fact, the scree from the Early Historic walls makes it hard to climb, but visitors can still trace the location of all the fort's major features. It is well worth the climb.

www.themodernantiquarian.com/site/712/
Excavation Report: http://ads.ahds.ac.uk/catalogue/adsdata/PSAS_2002/pdf/vol_120/120_095_149.pdf

Dunollie, Argyllshire

Built on the shore overlooking the modern port of Oban, the site of the Early Historic stronghold of Dunollie is now dominated by the spectacular ruins of a small 13th-century castle. In the Early Historic period this was the fortress of Dun Ollaigh, stronghold of the Cenél Loairn sub-kingdom of the Dal Riatan Scots. As such it was almost as important a fort as Dunadd. The castle is open to the public, and free access is provided by MacDougall Estate, who maintain the site.

www.obanargyll.com/dunollie-castle.html
http://canmore.rcahms.gov.uk/en/site/23027/details/dunollie+castle/

Dunnottar Castle, Aberdeenshire

Dunnottar Castle stands on a rocky promontory immediately south of the Aberdeenshire town of Stonehaven. Although the site itself is spectacular, the ruins of the medieval castle have obscured all visible traces of the Early Historic remains. However, it is well worth a visit, as it forms one of the most

Not all Early Historic strongholds were the same size. This useful diagram compares the size and layout of two Pictish forts (Dundurn and Urquhart) and two Scots' ones (Dunadd and Dunollie). The diagram also demonstrates comparative phrases of construction.

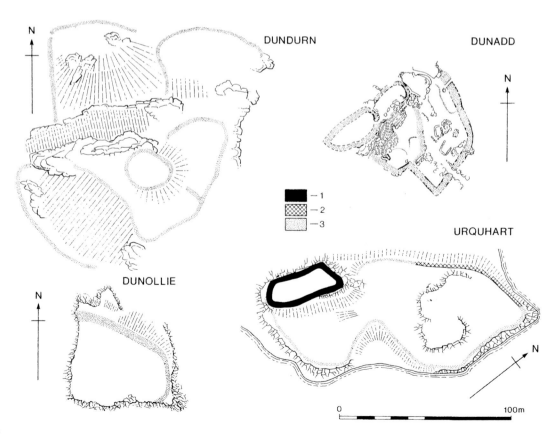

spectacular defensive promontory sites in Europe. The castle is run by Dunnecht Estates, and the site is fully open to the public.
www.dunnottarcastle.co.uk
http://canmore.rcahms.gov.uk/en/site/36992/details/dunnottar+castle

Moncreiffe Hill, Perthshire
The Pictish hill fort of Monid Craebe lies immediately south of Perth, and overlooks the M90 motorway. It can be reached by means of a forest path, and its summit provides spectacular views of the Perth countryside. The fort was shows evidence of several phases of construction, the latest of which is the large Early Historic ring fort or dun, which formed the central citadel of the stronghold. Access is free, although interpretation is limited, although the remains of the ramparts can still be traced.
http://canmore.rcahms.gov.uk/en/site/28025/details/carnac+moredun/

Portknockie, Aberdeenshire
The little promontory fort of Green Castle, Porknockie, still dominates the small fishing village, although little remains of the Pictish fort that once stood on its summit. The site lies on the coastal side of the village, and is easily accessible, although there is no form of interpretation available.
www.aberdeenshire.gov.uk/archaeology/sites/forts/greencastle.asp

Urquhart Castle, Highlands
Built on the shores of Loch Ness, and a prime 'monster-watching' spot, Urquhart Castle is one of the most photographed ruins in the Highlands. Unfortunately, the medieval castle was built on top of the remains of the Early Historic defences there, so there is no trace of the earlier structure there. However, the late Professor Alcock excavated the site, and his report (available online) provided visitors with the basics they need to interpret the Early Historic site. Urquhart Castle is owned by Historic Scotland, and is fully open to the public.
www.historic-scotland.gov.uk
www.undiscoveredscotland.co.uk/drumnadrochit/urquhart

Museums
National Museum of Scotland, Edinburgh
The museum contains some of the finest examples of Early Historic metalwork and carving in existence. This collection includes a substantial number of Pictish symbol stones, as well as other artefacts from the period. Finds from the Broch of Birsay and Dunadd are cared for by the museum.
www.nms.ac.uk

Pictavia, Angus
A visitor centre located just outside Brechin, which provides an engaging interpretation of Pictish history and culture. It also provides information that allows visitors to follow a Pictish Trial, a tour of several important Pictish sites.
www.pictavia.org.uk

Kilmartin House Museum, Argyll
This small museum offers an interpretation of the archaeological landscape in the surrounding area – which includes Dunadd.
www.kilmartin.org

Groam House Museum, Highlands
This small museum in the Black Isle village of Rosemarkie specializes in the interpretation of the area's rich Pictish archaeology and early history. It also contains an important collection of Pictish symbol stones, and other Early Historic artefacts.
www.groamhouse.org.uk

Other local museums and history centres, including Aberdeen, Dundee, Dunrobin Castle, Elgin, Forfar, Glasgow, Kirkwall, Perth, Portmahomack, Port Charlotte (Islay), Rothesay and Tain all contain small collections of artefacts relating to the Early Historic period in Scotland.

FURTHER READING

While there is no space to list the many useful archaeological papers which were consulted, many of them are available in most good libraries (particularly Scottish ones), and some are even available online. See Aitchison (2003) for a comprehensive list of the relevant papers. In addition the following books will be of interest:

Aitchison, Nick, *The Picts and the Scots at War* (Sutton Publishing: Stroud, 2003)
Alcock, Leslie, *Arthur's Britain: History and Archaeology, AD 367–634* (Penguin: London, 1971)
Carver, Martin, *Surviving in Symbols: a visit to the Pictish Nation* (Historic Scotland: Edinburgh, 1999)
Crawford, Barbara (ed.), *Scotland in Dark Age Britain* (Scottish Cultural Press: St Andrews, 1996)
Cummins, W. A., *The Age of the Picts* (Sutton: Stroud, 1995)
Driscoll, Stephen, *Alba: The Gaelic Kingdom of Scotland, AD 800–1124* (Historic Scotland: Edinburgh, 2002)
Edwards, Kevin, and Ralston, Ian (eds.), *Scotland after the Ice Age* (Edinburgh University Press: Edinburgh, 1997)
Foster, Sally M., *Picts, Gaels and Scots* (Historic Scotland: London, 2004)
Hogg, A. H. A., *Hill forts of Britain* (Hart-Davis Macgibbon: London, 1975)
Laing, Lloyd and Jenny, *The Picts and the Scots* (Sutton: Stroud, 1993)
Lowe, Chris, *Angels, Fools and Tyrants: Britons and Anglo-Saxons in Southern Scotland* (Historic Scotland: Edinburgh, 1999)
Nicoll, Eric, *A Pictish Panorama* (Pinkfoot Press: Brechin, Angus, 1995)
Ritchie, Anna, *Picts* (HMSO: Edinburgh, 1989)
Ritchie, Anna, and Breeze, David J., *Invaders of Scotland* (HMSO: Edinburgh, 1990)
Ritchie, G., and Ritchie, A., *Scotland: Archaeology and Early History* (Thames & Hudson: London, 1981)
Ritchie, A., and Ritchie, G., *Scotland: An Oxford Archaeological Guide* (Oxford University Press: Oxford, 1998)
Smyth, Alfred P., *Warlords and Holy Men: Scotland, AD 80–1000* (Edinburgh University Press: Edinburgh, 1989)
Sutherland, Elizabeth, *In Search of the Picts* (Constable: London, 1994)
Wainwright, F. T. (ed.), *The Problem of the Picts* (Nelson: London, 1955)

GLOSSARY

Bank	in terms of hill forts these are often associated with ramparts, although more accurately the latter represents the final bank before the inner enclosure. Banks are usually, but not always, built behind a ditch, from which the soil for the bank was excavated.
Berm	a flat space between the foot of a bank and the start of a ditch.
British	a collective term for the Celtic inhabitants of Britain during the Iron Age and Early Historic periods. In the context of this book they included the Gododdin and the Strathclyde Britons.
Counterscarp	the exterior slope or wall of a ditch, which in the case of hill forts was sometimes revetted using stone or timber.
Dun	a Celtic word for fort, the term usually refers to a small stone-built ring fort. The term is particularly common in western Scotland and Ireland. It is also found in modern Scottish placenames such as Dundee, Dunfermline and Dunkeld.
Early Historic	the period from around AD 213 when the Romans abandoned most of Scotland, until the end of the first millennium AD. It covers the period once popularly known as the Dark Ages, and can also be referred to by several other terms, including Late Antiquity and the Early Middle Ages, which it spans.
Earthwork	an earthen embankment, part of a fortification. In most cases a bank or rampart is classified as an earthwork.
Glacis	the slope extending down from the outworks of a fortification over which an attacker would have to move as he approached the fort.
Hill fort	defensive earthwork or stone-built Iron Age or Early Historic structure built on an easily defensible position, most usually the plateau or summit of a hill.
Iron Age	the period from around 700 BC until the Roman conquest of Britain in AD 43 when the inhabitants of Britain produced and used iron.
Multivallate	a fortification system where the central enclosure is surrounded by more than three sets of banks and associated ditches.
Promontory fort	a fortification built on a headland where three sides of the position were protected by the sea, leaving just one side requiring protection by manmade defensive works.
Rampart	in terms of hill forts and other Early Historic fortifications a rampart was the last bank defence before the inner enclosure of the fort.
Revetment	a timber or stone facing to a bank, ditch counterscarp or rampart, designed to protect it from erosion, or to impart additional strength to the structure.
Timber-laced	the archaeological term for a bank or rampart of earth or stone constructed around a timber frame.
Univallate	an Iron Age or Early Historic fortification system where the central enclosure is surrounded by just one set of banks and associated ditches.
Vitrified	the term applied to a stone-built Iron Age or Early Historic fortification where the stones were heated until they completely or partially fused together. This process imparted greater strength to the finished structure.

INDEX

References to illustrations are shown in **bold**.